The Lottery

by

George M. Hahn

authorHOUSE

1663 Liberty Drive, Suite 200
Bloomington, Indiana 47403
(800) 839-8640
www.authorhouse.com

First published by AuthorHouse 06/24/04

ISBN: 1-4184-7261-1 (e)
ISBN: 1-4184-4378-6 (sc)

Printed in the United States of America
Bloomington, Indiana

This book is printed on acid-free paper.

Acknowledgement

I am indebted to many people who have read my memoirs and whose suggestions have improved them immeasurably. In particular, I thank Les Gorn, Peter Greenberg, Lucie Buchbinder, Robert Starer, Tom Condon, William Drake, Jim Greenan, Mary Krainik, Beverly Paik, Evelyn Smart, and my wife, Joyce Hahn.

Table of Contents

Preface.

Memoirs always raise the question in the reader's mind: How accurate is the description of the events depicted and how much is contaminated by faulty memory? Almost all the episodes described in this volume occurred more than half a century ago. I would be arrogant in the extreme to proclaim that my recollections are so sharp that what I have written is a faithful representation of the way the incidents happened. I know only too well that memory can be tricky, and that impressions and 'facts' change with time. So I make no claims for absolute historical accuracy, if such a thing exists. What I have portrayed is what the years have made into a kaleidoscope of some of the experiences of my early life. Except to make sure that certain dates are accurate, I have intentionally refrained from doing any research about historical events, so that any errors reflect lapses of my memory.

Because I have a terrible habit of forgetting names, all the names in this book except those of my family members are fictitious.

September 1938: Friends.

In March of 1938 Austria was swallowed by its powerful neighbor. In August, shortly after the arrival of the German troops, Father was arrested by the Viennese police, turned over to the Gestapo and then sent to the Dachau concentration camp. He and his best friend were taking a walk near my parents' business when they were both picked up. We were fortunate in one way at least. We were rapidly informed about his fate. A policeman, an acquaintance of Father's friend, called his wife who in turn notified Mother. Others were not so lucky; for weeks the Gestapo and the police kept relatives in the dark about the fate of prisoners. We never found out whether the arrest was accidental or the result of a denunciation by a competitor, personal enemy, or a disgruntled employee.

Already at this early time, only a few months after the German take-over, nearly everybody in Vienna knew about the horrors that occurred in the camps. Even the children knew. In my class, in an academic high school near our flat, my twelve year old schoolmates taunted each other with: "If you don't shut up you'll be sent to a concentration camp. And you know what will happen to you there." I received a letter from a classmate. His father had told him that most likely I would never see mine again. The boy, Hans Weber was his name, wanted me to know that as a good Catholic he "would never have any to do with killing and torture." It was really a touching letter. Apparently he had once stolen some valuable stamps from me. He now returned them, and asked for my forgiveness.

What went on in the camps was one of the major topics of conversation whenever Viennese Jews met. Mother could not have escaped hearing about the horrible circumstances of the prisoners' daily existence. So the terrible impact Father's arrest had on Mother was hardly surprising. She started to have difficulties dealing with the day-to-day affairs of running the household. My fourteen-year-old sister, Lucie, had gone to a very different camp in Germany. There Jewish youths, thirteen years or older, were being trained for life in what was then British-administered Palestine. I was only twelve and therefore too young to accompany her.

By September, money had become scarce. Mother had put me in charge of selling off, among other things, our library. To get as much money for it as possible, I had decided not to take all the books to a dealer, but to sell them one by one. My parents had a large library. Mother revered books. She never had much formal education, and perhaps this increased her love and respect for the written word. The book collection contained works of the major German writers, translations of the best of the English and American works, also much of the French literature in its original tongue. As did many middle classes Austrians, my parents prided themselves on their ability to speak French. In addition, most of the important new works from many countries found their way into our massive bookcases. Friends or acquaintances were the authors of some of these books and their volumes often bore the author's signature and frequently also a dedication, usually to Mother. I don't know to what extent Father cared about books. It seems to me now that it was primarily Mother who relished them and read each and every volume.

The books were kept in large bookcases that were made of dark red cherry wood. They had glass doors, so that most of the books were easily visible even when the cases were closed. I liked to read the titles and occasionally pulled out a volume and read it. My parents never objected. I could read whatever books I pleased. The room where our library was located we called the bureau room, perhaps because it also contained a massive desk, also of cherry wood. It became my sister's bedroom; once my parents decided that we had become too old to share what until then had been 'the children's room'.

To sell our books, I had decided to place an advertisement in a Viennese newspaper, Die Neue Freie Presse. This turned out not to be as easy as I thought it would be. By October 1938, Jews were no longer allowed to advertise via public media, but I did not know this. Advertisements could not be placed by telephone, so I had to go to the building where that newspaper was located.

In front of the door leading to the business department there was a new, large sign. It announced that entrance to the offices of the "New Free Press" was strictly forbidden to Jews. I can still remember the shape of that sign and its colors. It must have been about three feet by two, although it looms even bigger in my memory. Heading it was a large black swastika on a red background. Most of the printing was in black except 'Juden' and 'strengstens verboten'. Those words were printed in the same strident red that matched the swastika background.

There was a policeman at the door. Perhaps his function was to scan all entrants to the newspaper offices to make sure that each was wearing a swastika emblem. Only Jews did not wear these. Even if they had wanted to, they were absolutely forbidden from doing so. It was the first such sign that I had seen in what was formerly a public place. By that time, nearly all stores, restaurants and other private places prominently displayed signs that announced that Jews were not wanted on the premises. These signs clearly represented the feelings of most Viennese, although at times the notices were there only to show that the owner of the establishment was not a Jew himself. I did not find such announcements particularly disturbing. They did not interfere with my life and did not seem much of a threat. While my occasional presence may have offended some storeowners, my money did not. Not once did anyone refuse me service in an establishment that proclaimed that it did not desire my business.

A sign that prohibited the entrance of Jews to a newspaper was for me a totally different matter. I had somehow always thought of the press as something special. Not that I carried any illusions about the freedom or objectivity of Viennese newspapers. I knew very well that what little autonomy that the press might have had in an independent Austria disappeared immediately when the Germans took control of the country. Perhaps because of Mother's attitude toward books, the printed word and the people involved in producing it had a special place in my thoughts. More importantly, the sign did not tell me that I was not wanted, but that I was not allowed. I clearly remember that for the first time the thought came into my mind that perhaps this is how it is going to be if I remained in Austria: not only would I not be wanted, but eventually I would not be allowed to exist. The presence of the policeman to enforce the edict added a particularly ominous note. Now no longer the expression of the prejudice of individual Viennese, this proclamation manifested the edict of the all-powerful state.

The sign frightened me more than I can ever remember, well out of proportion to the actual event itself. Thinking back now, I suppose that the fear was the result of the accumulation of many events. It started with the Anschluss itself, when I watched as the howling mobs of Viennese hysterically welcomed the Nazis. Then there was an incident shortly afterward when I had been dropping small, forbidden Socialist pamphlets in the streets of Vienna. I had joined what my parents assumed to be a Boy Scout group, but in fact was part of the youth group of the Austrian Socialist party that had been outlawed even before the Nazi takeover, ever since the civil war of 1932 between the Socialists and the conservative Catholic Party. A grocer's employee had chased and caught me. He thought I had been stealing grapes from the open display at his store. He was astonished when he opened my tightly closed fists, to find the small papers that prominently displayed the three red arrows, the emblem of the forbidden Austrian Socialist party. He relaxed his hold on me, and I quickly ran away. He did not bother to follow me, but I never participated in such activity again. The final and most frightening event was obviously the arrest of Father. I remember standing in front of the building that housed the newspaper, terrified, and made no attempt to enter.

The day that followed what I regarded as my failure, I asked the son of the concierge in our house to place the ad for me. Franzl was not quite two years older than I was. We had been friends for many years. He and I had lived in the same house all our lives. The two of us frequently played with toy soldiers in the garden surrounding our house. I had many of these, particularly Austrian cavalry miniatures. Father had been an officer in that body and frequently told tales about his adventures during World War I. My friend's father did the gardening in the large area behind the house, and also helped his wife with the cleaning of the interior halls of the apartment house. He had served in the infantry. I recall very little about him; he was a very quiet, unassuming man. Franzl and I staged large battles that lasted for many days, usually his infantry and artillery against my cavalry. In addition, we had a big secret in common. We regularly climbed to the top of the enormous walnut tree that grew next to our house, and then swung over from one of its branches to the balcony of our flat on the fourth floor of the house. This was at least fifty feet off the ground. Had either of our fathers been aware of what we were doing, we would have each received a well-deserved beating.

Our friendship went beyond this. On Jewish holidays, we frequently invited Franzl to our flat; Christmas Eve, and other days of Christian celebrations, I often spent with his family in their apartment on the ground floor of the building. We also shared a great passion. Jules Verne was our favorite author. I had received a complete edition of his works for my 12th birthday and Franzl and I were reading our way through each lavishly illustrated volume. We often discussed what we had read and agreed that becoming a

4

sub-marine captain, like the intrepid captain Nemo, would be a great way to spend one's life. Of course we also had our differences. For example, Franzl could not care less about politics. He thought that this was a dreadfully boring subject and knew and wanted to know nothing about it. I, on the other hand, at least in part because of the influence of our maid, was a confirmed and dedicated socialist at the ripe old age of twelve.

In view of our long time relationship, it seemed natural for me to ask him to go to the newspaper office. There was little or no danger in this for him. His name would not appear on any papers and there was no way to trace his participation in the unlikely event that someone should later complain about the Jewish advertisement. I told him that Jews were now forbidden from entering the paper's offices and asked him to do it for me. He immediately said:

"Why not? I'll do it tomorrow, after school. What's the ad? Write it down. Give me a piece of paper that has all the words. Also give me the money that it will cost. Don't forget the round-trip on the streetcar."

I knew Franzl would walk downtown. We always did that when we went to the movies together Saturday afternoons. Also, the office was not very far from his school. But I had no objections to giving him the extra few Groschen. That evening the doorbell rang and at the door was Franzl. I said hello and invited him into the flat.

"Everything go OK?"

He came in with a look on his face that I don't ever remember seeing there before.

"I went to the office of the 'Neue Freie Presse', but when I saw that notice I became scared. It is dangerous for me to help you get around the new laws, to fix things so you don't have to pay attention to such signs." The words sounded almost rehearsed. Franzl had never been one to worry too much about rules and regulations, so I was surprised to hear him now.

"Well, if you really feel you can't do it, just give me back the money for the ad and forget the whole thing."

Franzl's face changed to a look that now I would call sheepish, but then I did not know how to interpret.

"Well, I'll do it, Schurl, but you'll have to give me something." Not once in our relationship had Franzl asked me for anything.

"What is it that you want?"

"The volume of Verne that I am reading."

5

"What?" I really had a hard time believing what I heard.

Franzl became mad. "If you don't want to, that's fine with me. I don't have to help Jews." He quickly left and raced downstairs, but without returning the money for the advertisement.

I didn't know that Mother had been listening to the exchange. She came out of the living room into the hall, where Franzl and I had been talking. Mother started to cry, as she had done frequently in the past few weeks. She was clearly afraid. For herself, for me.

"I know how much you love these books, but does it really matter how many volumes you have?" she asked me.

I wasn't exactly pleased by what I considered to be a display of cowardice on Mother's part. It was only considerably later that evening that it occurred to me that she was losing her entire library that constituted such an important part of her life. Why was I making a fuss about losing one volume, even if it was a book by Jules Verne? So I went downstairs, and told Franzl that he could have the book. He took it and acted as if nothing had happened. The next day he placed our advertisement.

The books were indeed sold one by one. Buyers came to our apartment, also one by one. I had placed the books on tables, priced them by size, for lack of any better criteria. For those books that were autographed, I added a little extra. Sets, I insisted, could not be broken up. The people who came to buy were of all types. To most of them it was obvious that this was a Jewish family selling off part of its remaining possessions. Some tried to take advantage of this by offering prices that were ridiculously low. One or two even mentioned the illegality of my advertisement. Others attempted to browbeat me. To them a twelve-year-old could not be an effective adversary. But usually my youth was an advantage, and I really did not have many problems. Most of the books sold readily. Some buyers, I remember two, were openly sympathetic. One wished me luck, "no matter what happens", and the other shook hands with me after making his purchase and suggested that "God makes sure that good times follow bad."

In two days I sold ninety percent of what it had taken my parents fifteen years to accumulate. The money that I had taken in, I knew, was enough to feed Mother and me for at least three months. She had stayed away from all the transactions. During the day she was never home, but went to our store to attempt to run the family business, or visited various agencies to try to enlist help to obtain Father's release. In the evenings she went to bed very early.

I saw little of her during those days. After the sale I gave her the money that I had received. She didn't bother to count it but told me to take five percent for myself "as a commission". This I did and hid the money in one of my remaining books.

Several evenings after completion of the book sale, Franzl reappeared. He was wearing a Hitler Youth uniform, his Swastika armband flashing at me like a neon light. When I invited him to come in, he refused. I almost anticipated what he would say; though the tone was harsher than I had imagined.

"I saw that many people came up to buy your books. All because of the illegal ad. God dammed Jews are always breaking our laws or causing others to do so. You Christ killers really need to be punished. But…" Perhaps he was too embarrassed to go on.

"What exactly are you saying? What is it that you want from us?"

"If it were up to me, I would go to the police. But my father said that I shouldn't. Older people are full of sentimentality. I will not go to the police if you give me the rest of the Jules Verne books. You have until tomorrow to decide." He raised his right arm, yelled "Heil Hitler" at me and ran down the stairs without first looking at me. The next day he got his books. He and I never exchanged another word.

November 1938: Streetcars.

I had greatly underestimated my mother's strength. While she had troubles doing household chores, she worked indefatigably to attempt to have Father released from the camp. Mother requested an appointment at Gestapo headquarters in Vienna, but for many weeks there was no response. She appealed to veterans' and business groups, asking them to intercede, but did not even receive a reply. Then she wrote letters to former friends and acquaintances, non-Jews, asking them for help or suggestions. Very few responded, but old family friends in Berlin, non-Jews, did arrange for her to have an appointment early in November with the Gestapo in that city. Without hesitation she arranged to go to the German capital. I was left alone in our flat.

I had been alone for two days. On the third, when I woke up, the clock on the wall of my room, with its large arms and even larger numerals, told me that it was time to get up and get ready for school. The clock had been a gift from one of my many aunts. My toilet consisted of washing my hands and face, and quickly brushing my teeth. No one was at home to tell me that I had to change my underwear so I put on the same clothes that I had worn the day before. My sister was not there to tell me that my leather pants were beginning to stink, so I wore them. During the last few months before she left for the youth camp, it seemed to me that my pants were her favorite topic the few times she felt obligated to speak to me. I almost enjoyed the emptiness of the flat because it allowed me complete freedom to put on whatever clothes I felt like.

I could not see any point in making my bed, so I simply took my down-filled comforter and covered my crumpled sheets and blanket. Then I opened our front door and looked out into the hall to see if the Semmeln had arrived. The corner baker left these crunchy, white rolls nearly every morning. Usually he placed them on the mat in front of our door, but that day there weren't any. An absence of Semmeln was not exactly a rare occurrence, and it didn't worry me. The baker occasionally drank excessively. On those days when his alcoholic stupor interfered with his early deliveries, he called up Mother, or our maid while she was still with us, and complained bitterly that 'they' had stolen all the goods baked early that morning. Sometimes he told us who 'they' were: Gypsies, Poles or other foreigners, never Austrians. Most of the time it was just 'they'.

Not having found any rolls, I cut a piece of the good Viennese rye bread that we kept in a metal container on the large kitchen table, smeared it with butter from the ice box, jam from the cupboard and poured myself a glass of milk. Then I went to my favorite spot in our flat, the balcony. From that vantagepoint, our apartment was located in the hills surrounding Vienna, I could see much of the city stretched out below. In the summer, when the sun was out and the air clear, the view was really spectacular. The many green trees set off the gray and white buildings, the church spires towered above both. In the distance, in the center of town, I could clearly see the cathedral, the giant Stephans Dom and behind it stretches of the not-so-blue Danube. Even in November, on a cloudy morning, the city presented a sight that I did not tire of watching. Drifts of fog enveloped the taller buildings and the wind shook the trees that by then had lost most of their leaves. I thought that winter was on its way, and I wondered if I would be able to go ice skating, as I had done in past years.

I ate while reading a book that I had found hidden behind a row of tall volumes in my parents' library. The book was a sex manual, dignified in its medical descriptions, and I found its content fascinating. My terribly limited and skewed knowledge of sex was derived from comments made by my classmates and friends. Neither of my parents had ever mentioned the subject to me. It was not snooping that had led me to the monograph, but I had found it some weeks earlier, among the books that I had been selling.

The day before Mother had gone to Berlin, she asked my aunt Bertha, one of Father's six sisters, to call me every day to make sure that I was all right. The arrangement made Mother feel more at ease and the two evenings that my aunt had called I also felt relieved. I liked Bertha very much. She was Father's youngest sister and lived near the center of Vienna. She had never married and kept house with two other sisters, also unmarried. I heard later that there was some scandal about Bertha, she had an affair with a non-Jewish Austrian officer, but I knew nothing about this at the time. Nor would I have cared. If anything, it would have made her even more attractive in my eyes.

After I had finished my breakfast, I went into the living room and turned on the radio. Father had been in the business of importing and selling radios, so we owned an unusually powerful and versatile receiver. Even before the Anschluss, I frequently played with the set. The short-wave band interested me most and, after the German take-over, it became the source of all my political information. I particularly liked to listen to Radio Moscow. The words used by the announcer: Fascist pigs, Nazi murderers, Austrian bootlickers, Vatican stooges, all seemed to me to be objectively accurate in describing the world of Vienna that I saw. By contrast, the German language broadcasts of the BBC and the French emissions seemed to kowtow to the Nazis and hardly ever had any news that could be interpreted as anti-German.

Of course, it was dangerous to listen to a Russian station. I knew exactly on what wavelength and at what time the news was broadcast in German. Seven thirty in the morning, if I remember correctly, was such a time. After I had tuned in to the station, I turned the volume as low as I could so that, with my ear pressed to the speaker, I just made out the announcer's words. As an added precaution, I kept my finger on the dial so that in case the doorbell rang, I would not forget to turn to another station before shutting off the radio and answering the door.

The news was mostly about the Spanish Civil War and about another glorious victory that the government forces had just won over the lackeys of Italian and German imperialism. Even I was not too impressed. Radio Moscow recorded an endless string of Republican victories. Had they all been real and uninterrupted by fascist successes, which Moscow never reported, the war in Spain would have ended long ago with a Republican victory. I also remember that on that day the broadcast included an extended description of the horrors of the depression in the United States. Finally, there was a story of the assassination of a minor German consular official in Switzerland, or was it France? The announcer was not particularly interested. The killing did not seem to have been a politically inspired act, but only the deed of a deranged Jewish refugee. I paid little attention, but the broadcast also mentioned that retaliatory actions against Jewish properties had been taking place in parts of Germany and particularly in the former Austria.

After listening to the Russian news, I took my book bag with my school things and started to leave. I had to make sure that I had the keys to our flat, a piece of bread and some sausage for lunch. Then I went down our stairs. These were arranged in a helix, with two apartments at each complete turn. A railing made out of wrought iron separated the stairs from the central shaft. It was more fun to go on the wrong side of the railing where there was just enough room to get one's toes on each step. My book bag and lunch made things a bit difficult, but I managed to put one side of my suspenders through the handle of the book bag. When I then rebuttoned the suspenders, I only had to hold on to my lunch. As I worked my way downstairs, step by step while hanging on to the railing with my free hand, my book bag clattered against the iron. The clumsy rhythm of that noise sounded like a streetcar slowly moving over rails that had been worn excessively. It didn't take me very long to get downstairs, free my book bag, and run through the hall to the large gate that led toward the street.

In the small entrance hall, the concierge, Franzl's mother, was washing the marble floor. When she saw me, she got up and held out her hand as if to stop me.

"Schurl," she said quickly and quietly, "I wouldn't go out there today, if I were you. Terrible things are going on. All night, too."

I looked at her closely and to my surprise saw that she had been crying. I had never seen her like this before. I asked the obvious question:

"What kind of things?"

"For one thing, glass, it's everywhere. From the Jewish stores." She looked around to see if anyone could hear us, but we were alone. "The Nazis, the brownshirts, the SA, are breaking into the stores. They are beating people, good people that I know. The world is going crazy!"

"But I am supposed to go to school," was all I could reply. Whether I thanked her for warning me I don't remember. Probably not.

I went into the garden that was in front of the big iron gate, between the two wings of the apartment house. From there a small gate led into the street. As I looked out, everything seemed normal to me. People were walking as usual. Kids of all ages were on their way to school. An occasional car drove by. Then I overheard bits and pieces of a conversation from two passersby. What I heard sounded like:

"This will teach the goddamn Jews that they can not kill Germans anywhere."

I suddenly remembered what I had heard on the Russian broadcast. Whatever was going on, I began to realize, was, at least ostensibly, in retaliation for the assassination of the embassy official.

I was totally at a loss about what to do. Obviously the action was directed strictly against Jews. All Jews that the mobs could lay

12

their hands on, perhaps. I seemed obvious to me that the places to avoid where those where many Jews congregated. At the school I had recently been forced to attend there were only Jews. I quickly made up my mind that whatever I did decide to do, I would not go to class that day.

Would the Nazis come to our building? There was no way to know. Frightened, I started to return to our apartment. Just as I stepped into the hall of our building, another occupant of the house, a non-Jew, came down the stairs. Our concierge acted as if I were not there, but politely greeted the man. He quickly left without acknowledging me. She continued washing the floor, waited until the man was out of sight.

"That it should come to this! I would never…," the woman muttered to herself. She went on with her work, but now talked to me: "What are you going to do, Schurl?"

I had no idea what I could do, so I started back up the stairs. This time I used them the way they were intended. It seemed to take a long time to reach the fourth floor. My mind was going back and forth and in circles. Again I asked myself: would the Nazis come here? Were they going house to house to beat up all Jews? Were they arresting people? I knew that they had lists of the apartments occupied by Jews. Such information was available to them through the Viennese police. But then I did not know if this was an organized event or a spontaneous mob action. Because Radio Moscow already had knowledge of the happenings and their simultaneous occurrence in many parts of Germany made it sound like the former. Perhaps it involved only a few fanatics. I had a hard time believing that this was an organized assault on Jewish existence within Germany.

Inside our apartment I returned to the radio. Within a few minutes I picked up a French news broadcast. The major story concerned events that had happened during the night in Germany. In most German and formerly Austrian cities, well-organized groups of thugs had set synagogues on fire and broken their crystal windows. Vienna was singled out as having been particularly hard hit. Jewish stores had been trashed, individuals dragged from their homes and beaten, and hundreds if not thousands of Jews arrested. All this supposedly to avenge the killing of the German consular official. The French prime minister, was it Daladier or one of the other nonentities who were then playing musical chairs with French ministerial offices, had expressed his concern and the Quai d'Orsay, the French Foreign Office, was 'studying the situation'. There were pious statements from various other world figures, mildly or strongly condemning the German actions. It was obvious, though, that no country or group was going to provide any help. What scared me most was the report that bands of Nazi brownshirts were still going house to house, and again the announcer mentioned Vienna specifically.

A short time after the end of the French news, I heard the shrill tone of our telephone. Our phone was mounted on the wall in the entry hall. I quickly turned off the radio, which by now was playing Chopin, and started toward the hall. Should I answer the phone? What if it were brownshirted SA men checking to see if there was anybody in our flat? I doubted that it was Mother, since she would hardly dare to call from Berlin. My sister? Surely not. Finally, I decided if the SA men wanted to come here, they would hardly bother to telephone first. I took the receiver off the hook and answered.

I was vastly relieved to hear the voice of my aunt Bertha. Her tone was extremely agitated as she asked if I was OK.

"Things are terrible down here." The part of Vienna where she lived was home to many Jews. "I don't know," she went on, "perhaps they will kill us all…" She seemed to be even more scared than I was. "They are up in my flat. What, where can I… we go?"

As if I knew. "Where are you calling from?"

There was a pause.

"Public phone near our flat" was what I heard her say.

I did not know why I had asked this question. Then I had an idea.

"Why don't you get on the thirty eight or thirty nine streetcar and meet me at the stop on the Billroth Strasse on the corner of the Peter Jordan Strasse. You know the stop that I mean." It was the stop closest to our house. Bertha had been there often, every time she visited us. Perhaps as often as once a week.

"I don't know where. What are we…? Yes, of course I know the one. But why? What do you want to do?" I wasn't too sure myself. And I was beginning to be infected by her panic. I wanted to cut the conversation as quickly as I could.

"Meet me there in thirty minutes. Unless you can think of something better to do. And bring enough money. No, Never mind." How could she get money if she could not get back to her flat? Bertha agreed to come, obviously reluctantly, and hung up.

I cut myself another piece of bread, buttered it, sat down, got up, sat again and tried to think. As I chewed on the bread, it occurred to me that one thing that I could do was to look as normal and non-Jewish as possible.

I was already wearing my leather pants. I now put on some white knee socks, and a pair of shoes that I might have worn to a party. Then I took two of my parents' books that I had been unable to sell, and wrapped them in some festive looking paper. This was also left over from the book sale. In a drawer under the kitchen table our maid usually had kept all kinds of string. Luckily there I found a red piece of ribbon that looked like it had come from a birthday present. Several times I tried to tie a festive looking knot, but I was too nervous. Finally, I realized that if I were to meet my aunt on time, I had to leave. So I tied a simple knot. Then I took my book bag with my lunch, the books packaged to look like a present, and locked up the flat. I hoped that I looked like a kid who was going to school and then to a birthday party. What Jew would be crazy enough to go to a party on a day like this?

My walk to the streetcar stop was uneventful. We lived on a residential street. On it there were only two small neighborhood groceries and these were open as usual. I also did not see any signs of SA mobs, nor any evidence of damage to the few apartments that I knew Jews occupied. Perhaps things were not as bad as I feared. When I came to the main artery, the Billroth Strasse, things weren't that different. At first, I spotted no SA men or other suspicious groups of people. No one paid the slightest attention to me. The only store that I knew was owned by a Jew was tightly shuttered and had swastikas and anti-Jewish slogans painted on it. Such shuttered stores had become commonplace. Had I not been listening to the French broadcast, I might not have paid much attention.

My aunt arrived almost immediately after I came to the streetcar stop. She wore a skirt and sweater, had a bundle under her arm and carried her raincoat so that passersby could not tell whether or not she wore a swastika in its lapel. She did not want to advertise her Jewishness either. Bertha was a small woman, no taller than I was. Her eyes, blue like my father's, were circled in red, as if she had been crying and she wore a hat that covered most of her brown hair. She kissed me and then took a long look at my costume.

"This is not a holiday," was about all she said. We then started walking along the Billroth Strasse to the next streetcar stop, about three long blocks away. I carried my "present" so that it was clearly visible. I hoped that the pair of us looked like a mother escorting her son to school or to a birthday party. I proposed that we continue this role, but not do it while walking on the street. I knew that streets were not safe. After all, Father and his friend had been walking on a public street, when a policeman arrested them.

My idea was that riding the streetcars might be safer. Neither Bertha nor I had any hint that either the SA or any other Nazi band was checking passengers. If we looked sufficiently non-Jewish, and did not draw attention to ourselves, perhaps we would be left in peace. Just then, on the other side of the street a group of noisy SA men marched in their full uniform that included the ubiquitous swastika armbands. They were singing, laughing, and gave every sign of having a good time. One might have thought that they were on their way to or had just come from some particularly entertaining get-together. Luckily they paid no particular attention to us.

Aunt Bertha raised no objections to my suggestion. She was very pale and her eyes looked tired. She was probably so frightened by what she had seen that she was in a mild state of shock. I thought that she was relieved to turn decisions over to anyone, even to a 12-year-old boy. By now we had arrived at the next trolley stop. After a few minutes, a thirty-eight car came into view. That line went to Grinzing, a suburb best known for its wine drinking establishments. The car carried a large Nazi banner, as did many of Vienna's public transport vehicles.

Just as we were about to get on, I realized something terrible. In my excitement and fear, I had totally forgotten to take my money! In my pockets, I had only about one Schilling. The fare to Grinzing for the two of us was 70 Groschen. My money would take us to Grinzing, but not back. I felt terrible. Here I was beginning to think of myself as a big planner, but right away I had forgotten an essential to make the plan work. I felt like a fool, and very frightened. I told my aunt, who sighed and said that she had taken all the money in her apartment and that it would last us several days if need be.

We spent the entire day on streetcars, or waiting for them. From Grinzing we went to the Ring, the famed semi-circular boulevard that contains many of the city's most prominent and beautiful buildings. These, like most other public structures were now flying large swastika banners. Where we went from there, I have no recollection. I should not have been surprised, but my aunt knew Vienna much better than I did. She also turned out to be an expert on the city's transportation system. It was Bertha who decided what streetcars we should take and where we should get off to transfer to a different line. This often saved us money, because we could use the transfer coupons that the conductor issued at the beginning of each journey.

I was more than willing to have my aunt take charge. As a result, I paid little attention to what parts of the city we traversed during our Odyssey. Very likely, we attempted to avoid the districts that had many Jewish residents. Perhaps we, or really my aunt, chose lines that went long distances so that we would not have to change trains too often. We also never returned on the same streetcar that took us to the end of a line, but waited for a different trolley to make the trip back. Taking the same car might have aroused the suspicions of the conductor, something we certainly did not want to do.

I am really surprisingly hazy about the details of the day. I do not remember specific landmarks, nor can I visualize many faces of our fellow passengers. There are a few things I do recall clearly. We had lunch at the end of a car line while waiting for the return trolley. The trolley stop was covered and it had a bench. There were no other passengers waiting. I think it was drizzling or, at times, raining. The surroundings were bleak, unattractive and dirty apartment houses, very few trees. Very likely we were in one of Vienna's many poor neighborhoods. Exactly where, I have no idea. I offered Bertha part of my bread and sausage. Again my aunt surprised me. From her bundle she produced a box that contained some fried chicken, "leftovers from yesterday", bread, a bottle of a sweet, colored soda water, and two apples. Clearly, when she had realized that the SA might come to her flat, she had quickly gathered several essentials and left. I asked my aunt to tell me what had been going on in her neighborhood, why she had decided to leave so quickly. Her only reply was that this was nothing for children to hear. After that we ate our lunch largely in silence.

Twice groups of SA men entered the streetcar that we happened to be on. Once in the morning and again early in the afternoon. Neither group paid the slightest attention to us. In both cases the men were laughing loudly and talking about their experiences of the day and the previous night, as sportsmen might after a successful hunt. In the afternoon, the voices were louder and it was obvious that considerable drinking had been going on. On the wooden bench, across the aisle from us, a woman sat with her little boy, who was perhaps eight or nine years old. As the obscenities became louder and cruder, this woman smiled at my aunt and shrugged her shoulders as if to say,

"Well, boys will be boys."

That particular group of 'boys' was in the front of the car, mostly standing, while we sat about five rows further back. The streetcar was quite crowded, but many of their words were easily comprehensible. One particularly loud specimen talked about "a fat Jewish sow" that had been so frightened by his actions that she urinated on the floor. This was greeted with raucous laughter, particularly when the SA man described, in his thick Viennese dialect, how he had forced the shaking husband to lick up the mess.

I don't think that during the entire day we saw anything really terrible happening. If we did, I can't remember any of it. On all the business streets there were occasional shops whose windows had been smashed. Big signs were painted on the walls in front of these establishments. Some said simply: JEW. Others were more explicit: JEW, DIE. There was much glass on many streets and sidewalks. Men and women were cleaning this up. Later we found out that these were Jews forced to remove evidence of the damage that the Nazis had done to their stores and homes. Occasionally SA men walked or marched on the street, but in Nazified Vienna this had become a commonplace. More frequently we saw groups of people crowded around something, but we didn't see any details. For all I know now, these gatherings might have been perfectly innocent.

My overwhelming memory of the day is not one fear, but of dreadful boredom. I had not brought anything to read with me, another sign of my poor planning. Usually I did not go anywhere without a book. I did not speak much to my aunt because the things we wanted to talk about we couldn't, and obviously neither of us was in the mood for small talk.

I frequently dozed off, and then awakened as if startled by an unaccustomed noise. My 'present' and my school book bag were carefully positioned on my lap. I was worried that one or the other would slip off if I really fell asleep. I did not look at many passengers, because I did not want them to look at me. Bertha also did not sleep and tended to stare straight ahead, as if the bench in front of her contained a vital message that needed to be memorized.

We entered the trolleys mostly at the beginning of each line, so we usually had seats, even if the cars later became very crowded. Often I debated with myself whether to relinquish my seat to a woman standing near me, but I always decided against it. My biggest fear was that we would do something that would cause the other passengers to focus on us. Actually, I don't think that anyone paid the slightest attention. But we were never sure and I, at least, continually worried.

At about six in the afternoon we found ourselves at the end of the thirty nine line in Sievering, another suburb. From there it was not very far to our apartment. It had become dark. The trolley that took us there had been extremely crowded, primarily with people returning home from work. For the last hour or so we had not seen any groups of SA men, nor had we seen any unusual activity on the streets.

The part of Sievering near the terminal station consisted primarily of workers' homes. Among these was a group of housing complexes that the Socialist city administration built in the twenties. I thought of several acquaintances, members of my Socialist group that lived in the neighborhood. Among these were two men in their late teens that had continued to be active in the Socialist party, even after the Anschluss. One worked in a factory near by, and I thought that he would likely to be home by now. The other, when I had last seen him, had been out of work. He might or might not be home. Both lived in the same city-housing complex. Perhaps they would know what was happening.

"We can't spend the rest of our life on the dammed streetcars," I said to my aunt.

We were still walking near the station. The darkness had made us a little bolder. Bertha, who had definitely taken charge of things while we were on the trolleys, now returned to her earlier passivity.

"What can we do? I can't. . . They might still be at my flat. At your parents, who knows? I just don't know what we should do."

At this stage the only thing that I really wanted to do was not to ride on any more streetcars.

"I have some friends here. They might know what's going on. Or help to find out. Or. ." I really did not know what they could do, or, worse, if they would even talk to me.

Without showing any enthusiasm, my aunt asked if I wanted her to come along. We discussed that for some time and finally we agreed that she would stay on the thirty nine line, take it about half way to its end on the Ring, and then come back to the Sievering station. This should take about forty-five minutes. If by that time I had not returned, she should wait for me. It was unsaid, but understood, that if I did not show up in a reasonable time, she would be on her own.

The walk to the workers' housing project took about 10 minutes. I saw nothing that made me think that the daylong terror was continuing. I went to one of the entrances of the complex. Bullet holes and patchwork in the walls were vivid reminders of the civil war six years earlier when the Socialist and the conservative Catholic governing party fought for control of the city. The housing complex had been a Socialist stronghold and was heavily bombarded by government troops.

First, I went to the apartment where Hans, the unemployed, lived with his mother. It was she who answered the doorbell. The old woman did not know me and was quite suspicious. Finally, she did tell me that Hans was now working on the newly instituted nightshift of an automobile factory on the other side of Vienna. "So maybe things will be better for us from now on."

I agreed with her and went to look for Johann's small flat. I knew that he had recently married. Again I was not at all sure of the reception that I would get even if he were home. He had been involved in printing the small Socialist pamphlets that I distributed. He knew, of course, that I was Jewish.

When I found his door and rang the bell, it was Johann who answered. At first, he didn't recognize me in the dimly lit hallway on the third floor of the building. When he saw who I was, he grabbed my arm, and pulled me into the flat, and quickly closed the door.

"Na, Schurl, where are you coming from? What are you doing here? I am really pleased to see you." His wife, whom I had never met, came out from the kitchen into their one and only room. It smelled strongly of cabbage and other foods that I could not readily identify. I had heard that she too was a Socialist, but in those days political as well as internal loyalties changed rapidly.

Johann turned to her. "Liesl, this is the little one who used to help to distribute our material. I think I told you about the time he nearly got caught. Schurl with the tin hat." The last phrase referred to an old Viennese saying about George and his tin armor. She and I shook hands and then she put her arms around my shoulders. I was so relieved by the sincerity and warmth of the greeting that I nearly started to cry.

Johann was no fool. He quickly sensed my fear and anxiety. "I am sure you didn't come here to admire our wedded bliss. Anything to do with the Schweinerei that went on today? We are comrades, so if you need anything…."

I felt embarrassed. Nothing very serious had happened to me personally, and here I was appealing for help to somebody I really did not know all that well. I might even be endangering him. Perhaps he would consider the whole thing trivial and laugh at me. I explained the situation, that my parents were away and why, that I was alone in the flat and had been on the move all day to attempt to escape the raging Nazi bands.

"We …I need to know if things have calmed down and if the SA have left the building where I live." I had not mentioned my aunt.

Johann did not take what was going on lightly at all. He immediately got his jacket, asked me for my address.

"Yes, I know the street." He then kissed Liesl. "I have my bicycle downstairs. I should be back in 15 minutes. No, make it twenty. Liesl, perhaps something to eat." And he was off.

Liesl made me sit and brought me some bread smeared with fat and a slice of ham. "Do you eat this? I didn't think before I cut it." Perhaps even for her it was difficult to voice that I was Jewish.

"I am not religious. Of course I eat this, but … ". I didn't know how to tell her that I didn't want to eat the food out of their mouths.

Liesl sat the food in front of me. "You don't drink beer yet, or do you?" I didn't, so Liesl brought me some tea that she had just made. She sat with me at the table. I started to thank her, but she waved me off.

"The things that are happening. I can't believe… You know, we are quite religious, Johann and I. But now he is ashamed. To be a Viennese and to be a Catholic. What a terrible thing. I just… What's going to happen? "

I was suddenly beginning to feel very tired. The hot tea, with three spoonfuls of sugar, tasted wonderful. I did not know what was going to happen, and if I had known I certainly would not have told Liesl. She was far too nice to burden with knowledge like that. I said something meaningless to her, something like:

"I hope you won't have any trouble."

After I ate I looked at Liesl's face for the first time. She was not really pretty. Her eyes were blue, but her hair was a nondescript brown. There was nothing unusual about her facial features, a small nose, a modest chin. Her complexion was pale, and around her nose were a few freckles. In spite of her lack of comeliness I found her quite attractive; I particularly liked her kind smile and I thought that Johann was fortunate to have found somebody like that.

He came back a little sooner than the twenty minutes. He kept his voice low.

"The SA bastards have crawled back into their holes, it seems. I did not see any on the street. Your house looks perfectly safe. I went inside and heard nothing unusual. You'll be OK tonight. Tomorrow … who knows what…". He did not need to complete the sentence. It was obvious what he meant. I got up, thanked him and shook hands with both of them.

"I don't know how to repay you for this."

Both of them, almost in unison, waved me off. Johann finally said to me: "We should all get out of this goddamned country. It's gone crazy."

At the streetcar station, Bertha was already waiting. It was now after seven. We had to wait nearly 20 minutes for the next trolley to appear, and an additional ten before it started to move. Bertha agreed to spend the night at our apartment. She had tried to call her flat, but the phone was out of order. Perhaps it had been ripped off the wall. She also called one of her married sisters, Aunt Julie. The SA had invaded her flat and the brown-shirted rowdies had smashed much of the furniture and all the glassware. Luckily, nobody had been hurt or taken away. Apparently at Bertha's flat it had been a similar story. Julie had advised Bertha not to come back that night because there was really no place to sleep, and there were still a few men roaming the streets.

At our house there was not too much evidence of the day's activities. The doors of the apartments occupied by Jews, including ours, all had big J's smeared on them with black ink. Nobody had entered our flat. Apparently when no one answered the ring of the SA men, they just left without doing any real damage. All other Jewish apartments had been entered and the occupants terrorized in one way or another. The Nazis had taken one man away, but he returned late that evening, badly beaten. An older spinster who lived two floors below us was in bed with a broken leg when the brownshirts came. For many years her companion had been a beautiful and very friendly German Shepherd. The dog dared to bark, so one of the SA men shot the animal. The woman became hysterical and screamed for several hours before other occupants of the house dared to enter the flat and calm her down. She committed suicide a few days later.

The next day the J on our front door was almost gone. Early in the morning our concierge had come up and cleaned it off as best as she could. It was an act of bravery, for which she could have been severely punished. Bertha again called her sister Julie. Apparently everything was all clear, because she then went back to her flat. When she said good bye to me, she kissed me several times. She even felt mildly optimistic. "Perhaps, now that they have had their fill, this will be the end of the terror."

Of course it was not the end. For me the terror of that day remains forever in my mind. Nothing except death will ever erase it. For most of the rest of the world, it has almost faded from memory. But for Bertha and Father's five other sisters, the terror reached its end only after its ultimate expression in the Auschwitz extermination camp.

Nov.1938: Gestapo

Mother returned from Berlin two days later. It was about ten in the evening when she arrived home. She had spent many hours on the train without sleeping; part of the time she was forced to stand, and then took streetcars from the railroad station and finally walked the mile from the tram stop where aunt Bertha and I had started our trek. She was so tired out from her trip that we didn't speak more than a few words. After embracing me, she went straight to bed. It did not take me long to follow her example.

In the morning I woke around six. It was still pitch dark and I could hear rain falling on our veranda. It was too early to get up and I lay in bed thinking, worrying. The way Mother had looked the evening before had reminded me of the demeanor of tragic heroines of a few of the Hollywood movies I had seen. I thought that she could easily become seriously ill and I was not at all sure that I would be able to take care of her. All sorts of dreadful scenarios entered my daydreams. If she were to die what would happen to me? How would I eat? Where would I go? Finally, at seven, I got up. It was still dark and the rain was continuing its noisy performance. I heated some water for tea. To my surprise there were rolls at our front door. I also found some jam and a little butter in our icebox. The butter was nearly melted; the usual deliveryman had not brought ice in several days. I put all the food and some silverware on a trey and brought breakfast to Mother.

She was awake, but still in bed. Perhaps she sensed my extreme uneasiness, because she smiled and tried a little levity.

"The service in this hotel is very good." Her jokes were never very funny. I kissed her, embraced her and told her how relieved I was that she was back. She took one of the rolls, cut it open, smeared it with a little butter and jam and handed it to me.

"Here is your tip, garcon." Perhaps I laughed. Mother looked at me. "You should eat more; you are too thin." She didn't say what I should eat. She took one of the remaining rolls and started biting into it. No butter or jam for her. It was my turn to worry.

"And what about you? Shouldn't you eat more?"

Instead of an answer, she asked: "How did you like the three days alone?"

"They were not too bad."

"Did Tante Bertha call you?"

25

"Yes, she even spent a night here."

"That was nice of her. Did you thank her?" Apparently Mother knew nothing of the events that occurred only two days earlier. I only nodded and than asked about the visit to Berlin.

"I stayed with our friends, the Steinhardts. You remember, their son Jürgen, he is about your age. They were here with us only a few months before the Germans came. Their very nice house is in a suburb of Berlin, Dahlem, and we stayed there almost the entire time. So I didn't see much of Berlin. You know, they are really nice people. I was treated as a guest. It must take real courage now for a German Christian to have a Jewish house guest."

So that's why Mother didn't know anything about the events of the last few days. She had spent that time in the house of the 'nice' German Christians. I didn't want to hear anything about nice Germans. I didn't think that any existed. So I asked about the visit to the Gestapo.

"Herr Steinhardt took me. In his car. He had a written appointment slip, so we didn't have to wait, even though there were many people lined up outside, hoping to get into the building. The man we went to see was an uniformed SS officer. He was very polite to Herr Steinhardt, and even treated me with civility."

Mother ate the rest of her roll. She saw that I had finished mine and fixed me another. We both drank some of the tea, hers without sugar, mine with three teaspoons. I waited for her to go on.

"Unfortunately, the SS man didn't say anything encouraging. He did say that if we didn't have proof, visas and tickets, that the family could leave Germany, Jakob would certainly not be released."

"And if we do get visas and tickets?"

Mother shrugged. She was fighting back tears. "He said he was in no position to make any promises."

So the trip was really useless. And the nice Herr Steinhardt, how was it that the Gestapo treated him with kid gloves, even deference? He must have been in bed with the Nazis, yet he was kind and helpful to Mother. It didn't make sense.

The Nazis had begun to take over many establishments owned by Jews. Their method was to appoint an Aryan "business leader", usually an employee who was a Nazi party member. He then became the person in charge of the enterprise and its virtual owner.

Only a few days after Mother's return from Berlin a business leader was appointed for my parents' store; effectively it had been confiscated. In reality it was not much of a loss; it had not been making any money for some time. But the take-over did put additional stress on Mother. The man appointed as 'leader' was a seemingly mild-mannered, sandy haired former bookkeeper. He had worked for my parents for as many years as I can remember. During all that time he could not tell them often enough how happy he was in his job and how he appreciated working for the firm, and how much he liked my parents. They had no idea that during most of these years he had been a member of the illegal Nazi party.

Now this creature strutted around the store and offices like a circus master. He shouted orders at the other employees, all of whom quickly began to dislike him intensely. His particular pleasure was using his newly found loud voice to issue edicts to Mother. Usually he did so in front of others, presumably to demonstrate his authority. His orders frequently made little sense and sometimes were contradictory. Mother had to be careful. If as a result of one of these orders the business incurred losses, she would be blamed and could be forced to cover any possible outlays. Profitable decisions were due to the wisdom and business acumen of the 'business leader'.

This man took over Father's office and told Mother never to enter without his permission. I know that she suspected that he had fingered Father to the Austrian police. Perhaps he had. But a curious thing happened. After a few weeks of occupying the office, he no longer shouted at Mother, at least not very often, and told her that if she needed time off to 'straighten things out', he would not object. He once even mentioned that he regretted what happened to Father and that he 'never thought things would go as far as they did'.

The stories from the concentration camps became more and more horrifying. Killings there had become commonplace, at times for no reason at all, it was said. Although the winter was relatively mild, temperatures in Bavaria, Dachau is only a few miles from Munich, were nevertheless well below freezing. Tales started to circulate of prisoners loosing limbs to the cold, of freezing to death. Mother was forced to face the probability that she would never see Father again. She was prepared to stay in Vienna until he was either released from the camp or die there. Although my sister was attending the camp in Germany for young Jewish people hoping to go to Palestine, there was no assurance that the British authorities there would allow her to enter. It was at this time that she registered Lucie and me for possible evacuation to England or Holland, thinking that she might never be able to effect Father's release and leave Germany.

Not surprisingly, the accumulation of Mother's fears and worries, the possibility of not only losing her husband but her children as well, took its toll. She became extremely depressed and could barely manage each new day. Most household duties now fell on me. While I recall cleaning and shopping, and selling many of our possessions, I cannot remember who did the cooking. Perhaps we existed on bread, rolls, cheese, and an occasional piece of ham and simple dishes like a type of oatmeal that in past days we frequently ate for supper.

In the mornings our apartment was now empty. I was at school, and Mother was either in the office or following up some far-fetched lead that might result in the release of Father. The mailman usually came around 11 o'clock in the morning. He put letters under the front door mat. When I came home from school my first activity was to look at the day's mail. My sister wrote quite frequently; there were occasional letters from various relatives and once or twice even short notes from Father. Plus various notices about taxes, and bills for electricity, telephone etc.

One day, in addition to the usual mail, there was also a letter with a Viennese postmark, but with the imprint of the Gestapo. I tore it open immediately, fearing that it might contain the dreaded news about Father. Its content was short: "In the matter of the arrested criminal Jew, Jakob Hahn, you may present material on ...in room ... of the Hotel Metropol. If you do not appear on that date at the correct time, the appointment will be canceled." It ended with the usual greeting of the Third Reich: Heil Hitler! Even to a Jew.

I had heard about the Metropol. Before the Anschluss it had been one of Vienna's most elegant hotels. Its entrance hall was said to glitter with huge mirrors and impressive chandeliers hung from its ceilings. Its baroque decorations were a reminder of the Vienna before World War One when it was the capital of Europe's largest country and competed with Paris in matters of art and architecture. Only the richest tourists and businessmen could afford its tariffs.

Within days after the arrival of the German troops its clientele changed drastically. Huge swastika banners began to fly from its windows. Viennese police started to guard its entrances. Uniformed SS-men and sleazy agents in civilian clothes replaced the wealthy customers. The hotel had become the Austrian headquarters of the justly dreaded Gestapo.

When Mother came home from work, I quickly showed her the letter. As was now usually the case, she looked totally exhausted. Her face, even normally somewhat pale, looked ashen. Her eyes were ringed with black circles as if she already were in mourning. She sat down on one of the chairs that I had not been able to sell and started to cry. Her appearance really frightened me.

"How can I go there? You have to stand in line for many hours before they will even let you talk to them. And will it do any good? But perhaps it will harm him if I don't go. I am so tired!"

I did not know what to do. When I put my arms around her, she cried even harder, sobbing almost uncontrollably. She hugged me tightly, but continued to cry.

After some time it occurred to me that I might go to the Gestapo in her place. When I suggested this, she said that it was impossible, I was only a child, what would the Gestapo think of her and raised other objections while continuing to cry. I only pointed out that in her present state she could not possibly stand in line for several hours and that, in my opinion at least, I was hardly a child anymore.

When Mother finally was able to pull herself together, she managed almost a smile. "And to think that only a year ago I had to tell you not to throw snowballs at your sister."

She looked at me with her red eyes, still filled with tears: "Perhaps you ought to go. It may be that they will be kinder to a boy than to an old woman. Surely, even they won't hurt a child." It was the first, and I think the last time, that I heard her refer to herself as an old woman.

On the day of the appointment I got up early, before five, and took the necessary sequence of streetcars to the hotel. It was very cold and I wore my warmest clothes. Mother had said that I would have to stand in line for several hours and I wanted to be sure to have an adequate amount of time so as not to miss what was now my appointment. It was pitch dark and quite cold when I got off the trolley. At the hotel, however, several bright lights were shining, and, to my dismay, there were well over a hundred people already waiting. They formed a line in front of a gate, now tightly shut, and marked 'Jew Entrance'. A few Austrian policemen in uniform were walking guard.

Several older men were milling about the end of the line. These had what looked like medals pinned to their overcoats. As I neared the line, one of these, a stocky, short man approached me. Medals gleamed on his chest. He asked me quietly, almost secretively, if I needed to enter Gestapo headquarters and if I was Jewish. When I nodded to both, he switched to Yiddish, a language I did not understand. After I made this clear to him; he returned to his not very good German.

" For two hundred Marks I'll get you a place near the front of the line. It'll save you a very long wait." By mid-November the German currency had almost completely replaced its Austrian counterpart, the Schilling.

I had neither two hundred marks nor was I willing to pay this man.

"For a few hours' wait two hundred marks is much too much money." I did not want to admit that I did not have such a sum.

"A few hours?" The man shook his head. "You don't know what you are talking about." He pointed towards the front of the line. "Some of these people, or their relatives, have been in line for two days. And when they finally do get to the front there is no assurance that the police will let them in. The cops have a good time making some of the older Jews go back to the end of the line. But I was in the Army with several of them. If I give them half the money you give me they will put you at the head of the line and you will really have to wait only a few hours. Like the people in the other line, over there. For the Christians. They only need to wait a couple of hours at most."

Even in the dark he seemed to notice my disbelief.

"If you don't trust me, ask some of the people in line."

I did as he suggested and walked up to a man near the front of the line. A policeman eyed me suspiciously, but did not bother me. The man, perhaps in his twenties, told me that he and his wife had taken turns.

"This will be our third day. It's Father, you know. He was arrested two weeks ago. We have no idea where he is."

"Who arrested him?" I asked after I had told him that my father also was imprisoned.

"The Viennese police."

"So, why don't you go there and ask?"

"They won't tell you anything. They say only the Gestapo can give you information."

So that was why there were so many people in line. Now I did not know what to do. Two days' waiting would mean that I would miss the appointment. The Gestapo official, I was quite sure, would not be interested in any excuses. Further, without help, I knew very well that I could not last that long. I was devastated. If I did not appear it might even hurt Father's chances of being released. I might as well go home, I thought, there is nothing I can do here. I almost cried.

The bemedaled hero came over to me. "See, I didn't lie to you. Two days at least. That is surely worth 200 marks."

"I don't know where I could get money like that. And I have to get in there today. That's when my appointment is."

"I wish I could help you. I wish I could help everybody here. If we only had been not been born as Jews!" The man walked away, shaking his head.

I left totally dejected. How was I going to tell Mother!. I walked to the comer. The next streetcar came for the Ring; there I could get another car for home. I got on it. By now it was almost six, but the car was almost empty. I sat on one of the benches and started thinking. The words of the last conversation reverberated in my head. If only I were not a Jew I could get into the fast line. Then I thought: 'who would know that I was a Jew anyway?' I still had my student's identification from my school, almost pure Aryan; perhaps I could use that if I needed to convince a policeman of my German blood. I decided that I would ride the streetcars until about eight thirty. Then I would return to the Metropol and see how carefully the police checked papers. If it looked at all possible, I would try to get into the hotel by denying my Jewishness.

At about 8.30, I returned to the hotel. At a nearby kiosk I bought a copy of the Nazi party paper, the 'Völkische Beobachter'. I stood about a block away from the Aryans' gate, seemingly reading my paper but in reality watching the people enter. There was a short line that moved quite quickly. It seemed that for every Jew allowed into the hotel, at least ten non-Jews were admitted. The policeman guarding the short line did not seem too interested in the proceedings. Every few minutes he would motion the person next in line to go into the building. I screwed up every bit of courage I could muster, and approached the fifteen or so people waiting. I held my copy of the Nazi paper so that the large swastika on its masthead was clearly visible. The paper also covered my jacket so that no one could notice the fact that I was not wearing the Nazi emblem. Over the door of the gate was a large sign that said simply "No Jews". I almost turned away when I saw it, thinking of the consequences that my brashness could evoke. But then I repeated to myself what Mother had said: "Even they won't hurt a child."

So I joined the forbidden line. No one paid much attention to me. The policeman was now engaged in a conversation with a pretty girl and hardly looked at anybody else. Within less than an hour he waved at the man in front of me, indicating it was his turn. I quickly followed, acting as if we were with him. The policeman looked at me for a second and then waved me in also. There was no check of documents and I was in the building.

I don't know what I had expected to hear or see, perhaps shouts from the tortured, or bloodstained walls and carpets. But inside Gestapo headquarters all I saw were clean offices with people, mostly women, typing, filing papers and talking. Sounds of laughter came out of some offices; the smell of coffee pervaded the halls. Everything had the appearance of an ordinary government facility.

I had memorized the number of the office where my appointment was to be. There were signs on the wall and at the foot of the stairs showing me its location on the third floor. The elevator had a sign: 'Not for Jews'. I did not wish to press my luck, so I quickly ran up the stairs. Somewhere on the way I found a garbage can and deposited my newspaper. The name of the official I was to see was Obelheimer; His name was written in ink on a large piece of paper nailed to the outer door of his office. Perhaps he was new. I knocked, and a woman's voice asked me inside.

I handed my appointment letter do the secretary who was sitting in the outer office. She looked at it, made no comment and took it to the inner office. She came out a few seconds later and said,

"Wait", much as if she had been addressing a dog. Although there were chairs in the office, I did not dare to sit down. I just stood, leaning against a wall and waited. At least an hour and a half went by. I kept staring at the door leading to the inner office. It was padded with looked like carpeting that was decorated with small flowers. Several other people entered the room and these we quickly seen by Obelheimer. Finally a voice yelled "Hahn" and the secretary motioned for me to go in. I knocked on the door to the inner sanctum and an irritated voice told me to come in.

Obelheimer, at least I assumed it was he, sat behind a desk in the small office. He was bald, a heavy-set face, with a slightly reddish complexion. His blue eyes did not look sinister and he almost smiled at me when I came into his office. His appearance and initial demeanor reminded me of Father.

"You are here to talk about the Jew Jakob Hahn." It was not a question but a statement. "Are you related to him?"

"Yes sir, I am his son. My mother is ill and could not come."

Obelheimer almost smiled again. "And what do you want from me? You know your Father is no longer in Vienna. And I see that your Mother has already talked to Gestapo headquarters in Berlin."

"Yes sir." I behaved in a most respectful manner. Mother had carefully coached me.

"If my father is released from custody we will be able to leave Germany within a few days for the Dominican Republic, sir. But to get his entrance visa he needs to appear at the Dominican consulate in person." In 1938, the few Jews lucky enough to obtain visas to other countries were usually still permitted to leave.

"And we could get rid of a few more Jews. That would be good." Obelheimer then mumbled something that I could not understand.

I asked him to please repeat what he had just said. Obelheimer suddenly jumped up from his chair and yelled at me: "Are you deaf?" He used the Viennese expression 'terrisch"; no German he. He then slapped my face so hard that it brought tears to my eyes.

"Get out! And make it quick!"

I was stunned and scared and quickly did as I was told. In the outer office the secretary did not even look at me. The door to the hall was open and I rapidly walked to the stairs, down, and out of the hotel.

The cold air hit my face and stopped me from breaking into tears. I looked at the long line of Jews waiting. For what? An interview likes mine? How stupid they were waiting in line like that. Like sheep.

At home, I told Mother only that I had delivered her message. She did not seem to want to know any details about my visit and I did not offer any. Secretly I was proud of my successful deception. Cheating, lying and betrayal of one's friends seemed to be the best way to get along in the world that I was just beginning to know.

January 1939: Trains.

Today the train trip from Vienna to The Hague takes only a few hours. The route quickly crosses the border from Austria into Germany and then, near the town of Arnhem, into Holland. Border crossings are so smooth that passengers are hardly disturbed; a glance by border guards at documents, and sometimes not even that. If the crossing occurs at night, the conductor collects the passports in the evening, and there is then no need to wake the traveler. Between cities, meals ranging from simple sandwiches to elaborate feasts can be bought in the dining car. Youths from various lands, jaded by journeys to all parts of the world, now roam from country to country with a nonchalance that would have utterly confounded the traveler of the thirties.

Certainly this wasn't the way that my trip was in January of 1939. For one thing, there was no Austro-German border. Secondly, crossing the borders from Germany to The Netherlands required an exit visa from the German government and an entrance visa from the Dutch authorities. The former, at least in 1938, could be obtained, albeit at the price of relinquishing all real and most personal property. The latter, however, was available only to a lucky few.

In Vienna the Jews' situation deteriorated continuously. Anti-Semitism had been popular in Austria and much of the local population participated actively and at times enthusiastically in anti-Jewish activities. Towards the end of 1938, it had become obvious to all but the most obtuse that there was no future for Jews in what had been Austria, or for that matter in any part of Germany.

The rest of the world, however, had tightly locked its borders to the vast majority of German and Austrian Jews all looking for an escape. The very famous, the very rich managed to obtain the all-important visas stamped into their passports. These allowed them to enter other countries. A few long-time Communists found temporary refuge in the Soviet Union, but many of these perished later during the various purges instituted by the paranoid Stalin. For the vast majority of Jews, Germany became a horrifying prison. Emigration became almost impossible. Long lines of desperate people formed around each foreign embassy. America was the Golden Mecca. But even to be allowed to enter the immigration department of the US mission in Vienna required standing in line for many hours. Most of those Jews who did brave the line were then told that there were already so many would-be immigrants on file that the quota for Austrian-born men and women was filled for the next few years. The information at almost all other foreign legations was even worse. These countries were completely closed to the average Jew.

There were some exceptions. For those who had money, some things were still feasible. Latin American consuls and consular officials from some Asian countries were known to be approachable and, for ever-increasing sums of money, willing to issue the necessary entrance visas.

We had no money. Fortunately, we had relatives abroad, both in the United States and in Romania. These were doing everything in their power to help. The help took various forms. Strange individuals would appear at night in railroad stations, and give us packets that usually contained money, and sometimes letters to individuals in consulates of countries that I only recognized because of my stamp collection. I don't know how we could have lived without these gifts and the accompanying awareness that we weren't without connection to a saner part of the world.

The letters to the consulates, although we did not know of their exact contents, gave us hope that we might be able to leave Germany. Obtaining any visa took not only money but also time, however, and Mother was not at all convinced that Father would survive much longer. And even if a visa was obtained, there was no assurance that the Gestapo would then release him from the camp. She had made up her mind to remain in Vienna until, somehow, she could effect Father's release. Mother was fully aware that this might never happen and that as a consequence she herself might never manage to get out.

While she was willing to take her chances and remain in Vienna, she was not willing to have my sister and me share her fate. Perhaps more than most mothers; mine was convinced that her children were going to perform magnificent deeds that would greatly benefit humanity. She saw it as her duty to make sure that we would not disappear in the abyss that she foresaw as developing in Germany.

Feeling as she did, it was hardly surprising that when she heard about the English and Dutch programs, she investigated these and signed us up immediately. This turned out to be a wise move. By the time the transports actually started to leave Vienna, there were far more applicants then the host countries were willing to accept. So children were chosen based on the date that their parents had signed the necessary documents. For one of the early transports to England, Lucie's and my name came up. We were at the very end of the list, so that there was room for just one of us. My sister was the older and therefore the first choice to go. Further, she was anxious to leave Germany. She had become an ardent Zionist, and hoped that getting to England would be the first step that would eventually take her to what was then Palestine.

I was not really looking forward to leaving Vienna. At the time of my father's arrest, my life had not changed excessively. I still went to the same Gymnasium that I liked and had attended for the past two years. Jews now had to sit in the last row during class, and were excluded from the games that went on during each recess. But otherwise we were not bothered. Most of the teachers treated us fairly. There were of course exceptions. My German language teacher, for example, had always vociferously proclaimed his allegiance to the Austrian State. This toady creature now always sported a large swastika in his lapel and never missed a chance to stick out his arm and loudly yell "Heil Hitler". He also quickly became the most active Jew-baiter. For us it became difficult to get a passing grade in his class.

By contrast, several other teachers behaved normally and treated all students alike. This even included some who, as all the students knew, had been 'illegals', members of the Nazi party before the Anschluss. Towards the end of my last term at the Gymnasium one of these, my math teacher, asked me if I wanted a B, or an A and a slap in my face (eine Ohrfeige, a fig on the ear, was the Viennese expression that he used). I chose the A. True to his word, I immediately received a blow to my cheek, and later an A on my report card. I knew exactly why he had hit me; my frequent talking in class must have irritated him to no end. Although I knew that he was a Nazi, he was one of my favorite teachers and he continued to treat me the same way after the Anschluss as before. Some of the non-Jewish students taunted us, but on the whole we had surprisingly few problems.

I also felt that I was useful to Mother and that she needed me. After our maid had reluctantly found a position elsewhere, it fell upon me to take over many of her chores. To my surprise, I enjoyed the daily routines of cleaning and shopping. In short, I didn't then see any reason for me to leave Vienna.

This situation did not last long. My sister went to England in August of 1938. In September, the Vienna school authorities decreed that one public school was to be exclusively for Jewish boys, another for girls. None of us could attend school elsewhere. Suddenly my life was transformed. I knew very few of my new classmates. The teachers in the new school considered their new assignment both temporary and degrading. They behaved accordingly. While in my old school it had taken me about 15 minutes to walk to class, now it took about one hour. But these were minor problems. Much more troubling and painful was the development of a new sport among the Viennese youths: hunting Jewish children. After school we were frequently attacked by bands of older boys.

At first these waylaid us at irregular intervals several blocks from our school. They waited until we had separated and were walking in groups of no more than two or three. Then five or ten of them, usually wearing Hitler Youth uniforms, would jump us, hit us a few times and then disappear rapidly. When it became obvious that neither the school authorities nor the police had any intention of interfering, the gangs became bolder and the severity and length of the beatings increased. Not that any of us were seriously hurt. A few bruises, an occasional black eye. These drubbings did however become more than a nuisance. We tried all means of escaping the attacks; running and varying our routes, going singly or in groups, but nothing really worked. Mothers came to escort their children. But even this frequently did not help. While the Mothers were not physically attacked, they were prevented from coming to the aid of their offspring. Many times adults witnessed these attacks, but I can remember only a few rare instances when a Viennese made any attempt to stop the beatings. Some just watched and others, including women who must have had children of their own, cheered. In October, attacks on Jews in Germany intensified; the culmination was the Kristall Nacht. The message of the attacks was clear: Get out of Germany at all costs. We also learned that Father had been transferred from Dachau to a different camp, Buchenwald. Its reputation was even more horrifying than that of Dachau.

Because of these events, when in December of that year a place became vacant for me on a transport to Holland, I raised no objections. I had reached the conclusion, wrong as it fortunately turned out, that Father would never be released from the camp. Mother, I imagined, would stay in Vienna until it was too late. I did not share my sister's wish to go to Palestine, but secretly harbored the illusion that once I left Germany, it would be easy for me to make my way to Spain and there to join the Republican armies then fighting the Nazi-backed insurrection of the Franco forces.

The office in Vienna that handled details of the children transport was run by a group of Quakers, primarily from Great Britain and the United States. These gentle, generous people had to make daily decisions that involved matters of life and death for Jewish children. Obviously, most of them had not expected anything of the desperation and panic that they encountered. Many responded magnificently to a task that required wisdom that frequently would have taxed a Solomon and patience that was too much to ask of anyone. Others retreated behind strict interpretations of the rules. It was well known in Vienna, however, that the Quaker-run offices were oases where even Jews were still treated as human beings.

The day of departure of my transport was a Wednesday. We were told to assemble in front of the principal Vienna railroad station at seven in the morning. Each child was allowed to bring one suitcase and a package to take on the train. All of us were accompanied by our mothers; fathers had been urged not to come, probably out of consideration for their own safety. Most of them arrived anyway. The children ranged in age from about four to fifteen. Nearly everybody was in tears. The mothers were trying to keep their extreme grief from infecting their children. The fathers continually used handkerchiefs to hide their tears. Parents picked up their children intermittently, hugged and kissed them with desperate intensity. The reaction of the children varied with age. The little ones cried inconsolably. Those older, perhaps about ten, also cried a lot, but they could, at times at least, be bribed by pieces of chocolate or other candies. Others, my age or older, tried to maintain an indifferent appearance. Most of the time we, too, were unsuccessful.

Mother held my hand and did not let go for at least an hour. She had brought a bag of sandwiches with her and kept urging these on me. My stomach did not feel like food. I kept saying to myself: "Look carefully, you might never see her again." I tried to think of something to say that might reassure her but I could think of nothing. When she offered me a sandwich once more, I became irritated. "I am not a baby. I know when I am hungry." I did not dare to look at Mother's face.

We had to lineup in alphabetical order to have our passports, consent papers, Dutch visas etc. checked. I remember the two children behind me, Heinz and his older sister, Eva. Their parents walked with them. No words were exchanged between parents and children, but their hands were in continuous communication. One minute the father would wrap his arms around his daughter's waist, the next minute he was stroking his son's head and shoulders. The mother held on to the children's hands most of the time. Occasionally she would turn to the father and touch him. To give or to receive courage?

In front of me a mother was carrying her 5-year-old daughter. They seemed to be talking to each other continuously. Apparently the family had relatives in Amsterdam. The mother kept telling the girl how wonderful it would be to see aunt Ingeken. She invoked past meetings, descriptions of good things to eat, and told about the wonders of the ocean and the beach. But the child would have none of it. She kept thinking of more and more reasons why she should not leave. "How will daddy know how to find me?" was followed by "kitty needs me" and "But I have more aunts here, so its better to stay here than go to aunt Ingeken". The mother finally stopped talking, embraced her daughter and held her tightly until they reached the desk where papers were checked. Parents were not permitted beyond that point. The screaming girl was taken to the train by one of the young women who later accompanied us to Holland.

The train was scheduled to leave at 10:00 in the morning. By that time all our papers had to be checked and we were seated in special cars attached to the regular train going to The Hague and Amsterdam. There were between 100 and 200 children in four or five railroad cars. One girl did not make it. In the last minute her parents could not part from her.

As I said before, parents were not permitted to enter the track from which the train departed and of course thereby were prevented from boarding the train. I said good bye to Mother, kissed her and watched as she walked away. She then turned to wave at me. She was by then quite some distance away. Perhaps she thought that I could not see that she was crying.

I don't remember who assigned us to our seats; perhaps it was done alphabetically. The train consisted of regular 3rd class cars. These were divided into several compartments. Two wooden benches lined each of these. There was room for ten children in each compartment. In my group their ages ranged from about 4 to 12; Eva, the girl that had walked behind me was the oldest. Perhaps

I was next. At first we were all very quiet. It seemed hours until the train started to pull out of the station. I suppose we were all thinking about our families, about leaving home. The younger children started to examine the contents of the packages they had brought with them. A few dolls appeared and pieces of candy disappeared into the mouths of the little ones. Eva took on the role of den mother and comforted the periodically crying children as best she could. Not all the children behaved the same way. One boy, perhaps 5 years old, sat down on his part of the bench and almost immediately fell asleep. His eyes remained closed for several hours. Some of the older children surely worried about the uncertainty of the future.

I can clearly recall the book I was reading at the time, but of my thoughts during the period of waiting my memory refuses to speak. All I distinctly remember is a sense of relief when the engine started to make loud hissing noises, the train jerked a few times and then, with slowly increasing speed, began its forward motion.

Although our train had an international destination, it was not an express, and stopped at many small towns. I did not recognize most of the names and do not remember them. In one town the children's cars were uncoupled from the rest and left standing on a siding for what may have been as long as a few hours. We were then attached to a short freight train and continued our journey across Germany. Swastikas were everywhere; in every station there was at least one large banner and, as we moved through towns and villages, we saw others fluttering from what probably were municipal buildings. Uniforms were a common sight. Wehrmacht soldiers, Hitler youths, police, railroad employees, soldiers, the brown shirted SA men and, occasionally, the frightening, sinister looking black shirted SS constituted part of Germany's everyday scene. At times on the highways we saw groups of uniformed men marching in formation or soldiers in endless lines of motorized vehicles. It seemed obvious to me that this was a country preparing for war. In the Third Reich, no one could escape the omnipresence of the regimentation that increasingly reached into all aspects of the society. The uniforms and flags that we saw everywhere were continuous reminders of this horrifying process.

The day dragged on. We were given sandwiches: pieces of stale bread smeared with either peanut butter or jam. The Dutch refugee committee supplied these. I hated the taste of the slightly spoiled peanut butter, something unknown to us spoiled children. The other children seemed to feel the same way. These sandwiches remained uneaten. Most of us had enough food from packages carefully put together by parents. Included in my provisions were fried chicken legs, cold pieces of Wiener Schnitzel, large pieces of Viennese bread, and apples, pears and even an orange. How Mother had managed to accumulate all that food was a mystery to me. With the food that we had brought and the jam sandwiches no one went hungry. We all shared whatever we had, except that some of the younger kids insisted on eating all their candy.

A sign that I did recognize announced that we had arrived in the suburbs of Frankfurt on Main. I was quite excited when I read this, though somewhat puzzled. I did not think that Frankfurt was on the direct route between Vienna and the Dutch border, but I was not sure. Anyway, who understands the vagaries of railroad systems! Frankfurt had always impressed me as the most interesting of German cities. It had the reputation of being the most liberal and tolerant. Its history as a mercantile center was only exceeded by its cultural fame. I remembered from school that Goethe, Schiller and Heine had contributed to its literary past; and that Schumann, Mendelsohn and Brahms all had lived at least part of their lives in this enlightened city. It had a famous university and its newspaper had at one time been regarded as one of the world's great. Berlin may have been Germany's political capital, but Frankfurt was its cultural fountainhead. I was looking forward to getting at least a glimpse of this great city that represented the best of German culture.

Our train stopped at a small station in the outskirts of town. The platform closest to our train teeming with brownshirted figures carrying banners and shouting loudly. The banners carried anti-Jewish slogans: down with Jews; Juda verrecke (die, Jew), Jewish pigs get out of Frankfurt; the new Germany does not want live Jews. Those yelling were primarily young Hitler Youths, though a few older men wearing the brownshirts of the SA were also visible. Soon their activity was no longer restricted to yelling. Bottles and stones were hurled at the train. Rapidly most of the windows were broken, and glass was flying in all directions. The 4-year-old girl in my compartment started to scream hysterically. A small piece of glass had cut her face and she was bleeding slightly.

Although I was stunned at first, I did have enough presence of mind to grab the girl, and place myself over her so that she was protected from the flying missiles. I tried to calm her, but was not too successful. I also noticed that Eva similarly was protecting one of the other small children. The other younger children all began to cry and scream with fear. Eva and I motioned for them to get on the floor. Their voices intermingled with the sound of breaking glass and the howling of Frankfurt's youths. My body was shaking with fear and rage and utter helplessness. I tried to think of something to do, but there was nothing but to lie there and wait for events.

Nothing else, however, happened. The engine started up again, the train moved forward and out of the range of the stones and bottles. The whole episode could not have lasted more than 5 minutes and perhaps even less. Then it was all over. The little girl under me started to calm down. The screams of the other children became sobs and the noise of the platform crowd was drowned out by the reassuring noise of the train's motion. I looked at Eva and noticed that she was crying.

I don't know what happened to the adults on the train. I imagine that they were busy with some of the other children, although we found out later that fortunately nobody had been seriously injured. It fell to Eva and me to try to calm down the younger children. They demanded their parents, and sobbed and cried for quite some time. It was also beginning to be bitterly cold. On one side of the train nearly all the windows had been broken. Even on the side away from the platform, several of the panes were either completely gone or had cracks or holes in them. As the train gathered speed, the cold winter wind blew through the compartment. In a way this was a blessing, because it distracted the children who now started to go through their belongings to find sweaters and coats.

The only child that had received any injury in our compartment was the little girl that had been cut by flying glass. Eva used one of her handkerchiefs to make a makeshift bandage for the wound. It was really just a minor cut, but it had certainly frightened the child. Another boy and I cleaned up the broken glass as best as we could, so that at least the benches became safe for us to sit on. There was still much glass on the floor and we had to make sure that none of the small children took off their shoes. Eva and I checked to see that all the young ones had put on sufficient warm clothes. Then we both sat down and fell asleep from exhaustion.

The rest of the trip was uneventful. The border crossing went smoothly; neither the German nor the Dutch border guards entered our compartment, nor to my knowledge any of the others. Perhaps there was too much glass on the floor. We arrived in The Hague in what seemed to be the middle of the night. There we were taken by bus to a temporary shelter.

There was, however, an aftermath to these events. We were told by some of the nurses who took care of us in the camp, that the refugee committee had received a letter from the German railroads complaining that "the vandalism carried out by the Jewish children, particularly the breakage of glass, was so extensive that the railroad might no longer provide service to the committee. Further, the damage done will have to be paid for. Bills will be sent to the parents of the children to make certain that the German State does not suffer any losses from this outrageous Jewish behavior."

I don't know if Mother ever received a bill, or if she did, if she paid it. But the technique of charging the victims became part of the railroad's policy. Some years later, Jews from all over Europe were transported in cattle cars of the German railroad system to the death camps in Poland. The Jews themselves had to pay for the trip whose final destination was their own extermination. But, in a gesture of extreme fairness and generosity, the German railroad only charged them for one way tickets. And, presumably, children under the age of twelve were transported for half price.

Winter 1939: The Park

For a few days after our arrival in The Hague we were housed in a large building in the center of town. It may have been part of a hospital because there doctors examined all the newly arrived children. We expected then to be placed with individual families. But things turned out differently. The morning after our arrival, one of the members of the Dutch refugee committee joined us at breakfast. After we had finished eating, she stood up, and asked for our attention.

"There has been a change in plans," she announced. "You will not be sent to individual homes, In a day or two you will go to different camps. Perhaps camp is the wrong word. Different hostels. You will be in groups, so you won't feel lonely. We have picked out some very nice places for you."

There was not much reaction to her announcement. I think that many of the children were quite relieved by what she had said. I certainly was. The idea that foster parents would take me in sounded too much like replacing my real ones. I was, however, curious to know why plans had been changed. Perhaps, I thought, there were not enough volunteers to take us into their homes. But at the time I was too shy to ask either the committeewoman or any of the nurses that staffed our temporary shelter.

I found out much later that in the fall of 1938 the Dutch government had granted permission for a small number of German and Austrian children to enter The Netherlands. This did not entail too much political or economic risk for the Government. The time had not yet come for the Nazis to admit openly that they were out to erase Jews from the face of the earth. The term Judenfrei (free of Jews) was only coined in the 1940's. It was the Puppet State of Croatia, created by the Nazis during World War II that first claimed that terrifying appellation. In the days before World War II, Germans were still somewhat sensitive to international public opinion. Interfering with the removal from its clutches of a small number of children might have shocked even Nazi sympathizers within and without Germany.

On the economic side, the Dutch government was not asked to provide any help. A committee of private Dutch citizens made all arrangements for the care of the children. This group consisted primarily of Dutch Jews, although many non-Jews contributed actively to its work. This committee agreed to be responsible for all costs associated with the transport of the children and their subsequent maintenance within the country. There were many Dutch citizens, Jews and non-Jews, who were appalled by the reports of German atrocities as reported amply by the left of center press. As a result there was no shortage of volunteers willing to open their homes to one or two children and do so for as long as required.

But somebody in the Dutch government objected. The Nazis might not look kindly upon temporary adoption of Jewish children, particularly by non-Jewish Dutch citizens. They might interpret such action as proof of Dutch anti-German sentiment. And nothing must be done to offend the powerful neighbor. So, instead of being placed into private homes, we were to be housed in camps.

We were divided, I don't know according to what criteria, and bussed to more permanent quarters. For me, and for several of the recent arrivals from Vienna, our new abode was a park on the outskirts of the capital. Even in the middle of winter, the grass there was lusciously green; the winter had as yet not been cold. On the day we arrived it rained, but occasionally the sun broke through and then the raindrops on the bare branches of the many trees reflected and dispersed the sudden bursts of light. Clumps of various bushes whose names I did not know dotted the park, and there were ponds inhabited by swans. These were clearly visible from the bus that carried us.

The road in the park led to a two-story building located on a grass-covered knoll. The structure was painted an inviting white and even from the distance I could see a large veranda that extended along much of the second floor.

"I bet the view from up there is quite something," I said to the very quiet boy, he was about my age, who sat next to me.

"Perhaps." His mind was obviously on other things.

"No wonder the woman had told us that the committee had picked out some nice places," I thought to myself. "This looks more like a vacation hotel than a camp." Our busses drove to the side of the building. Here, however, the paint was old, peeling off in places. The building had seen better days. As we climbed out of the vehicle, we were met by four or five women wearing the traditional habits of Catholic nuns and by the mildly curious stares of other refugee children. Their arrival, from various parts of Germany, we learned later, had preceded ours by several weeks.

The nuns called out our names and, one by one, we were led through poorly lit and unheated halls to our barrack-like dormitories of our abode. Mine, and that of five other boys, was a large room on the second floor. The room had recently been painted white; its only decoration was a large picture of the Dutch queen. But it had two windows that overlooked the park and a door that let out to the veranda that I had seen from the bus. In front of each bed was a wooden box. It was big enough to hold our belongings, as each of us had brought only one suitcase and perhaps a small bag that contained a few extra things.

Shortly after we had deposited our luggage, the nuns herded us newcomers into a hall that was barely heated even on this cold and wet day. It contained many large tables lined with chairs. Eating utensils, dishes, cups and silverware filled a large counter that lined one of the walls. All the windows were closed, and an unpleasant dampness and musty odor of stale food pervaded what was obviously the dining hall.

The nuns told us to sit around two of the tables. We did so quietly. None of us knew what to expect, and even the younger children were subdued in this undecorated and chilly room. I felt a distinct letdown as I contrasted the excitement and pleasure that I felt when the bus entered the lovely park with the forbidding surroundings of the interior of our new home. The difference seemed to underscore the worry many of us felt about the uncertainty of our future. A little girl sitting across the table from me said to no one in particular: "It stinks in here." Her face had such a sad expression that I thought that she would burst into tears any second.

But the mood of children changes quickly. Two of the older girls who had been in the camp for some time wheeled a large pot into the dining hall. They, and some of the nuns, filled cup after cup with hot cocoa and passed these to us. The girl across the table, perhaps 6 years old, laughed happily, as she tasted the sweet liquid.

While we were still occupied with our treat, two new nuns came into the room. One was middle-aged, possibly in her forties; the other appeared to be much younger. I thought that she wasn't much older than I was, though that proved to be quite wrong. The older nun walked rapidly with an almost military gait that was in strange contrast to the softness of her flowing habit. She climbed on one of the chairs and addressed us in passable German. Her name was Monika, she said, and she was in charge of the camp.

She welcomed us, though with barely a smile, and then told us that she knew how difficult it was for us to have left our parents and to be away from home and from all our familiar surroundings.

That was all the sentimentality. Sister Monika then went on to describe the running of the camp. We were expected to do all the work that related to serving meals, washing dishes and clothes and keeping our rooms clean. There were to be work details for those of us ten years or older. "Sister Emmetta," she pointed to the young nun who seemed to have a constantly worried look on her face, "will make assignments. Not today. You have seen your rooms and beds. Unpack your belongings, and then you are free to do whatever you want. I am sure some of the children that have been here for some time will show you around. Work assignments will be done tomorrow. The work is not difficult, and I expect each of you to do your part without complaining". She repeated her welcome without wasting a single word, stepped off her chair and brusquely walked out of the room.

But complaining started immediately after we had put away our belongings. Some of the children criticized our accommodations, and not a few expressed surprise and dismay at the tone of our welcome. Obviously, Sister Monika had not struck familiar strings. None of the niceties of Viennese hypocrisy; none of the cloying sweetness of Jewish parentage.

Some of the boys were particularly upset. "Such work is for servants or girls. I don't want to do any." "I didn't have to clean at home; why here?" Most of the protest was about housekeeping. In homes of middle class Austrians, Jews and non-Jews alike, maids did the scrub work, and frequently the cooking as well. The poorer Jewish children came primarily from orthodox homes. There only women and girls were expected to do housework. "How can Christians, particularly Catholic nuns, have any understanding of Jewish tradition?" one older boy questioned. Others picked up on this theme. Soon some of the orthodox children were voicing the fear that attempts would be made to induce or perhaps even force us to become Catholics. This became almost a panic. One of the smaller boys, whose orthodox background was attested to by the Yarmulke he wore, started to cry: "I don't want to become a Catholic."

Fortunately, by then several of the camp's veterans had joined us. These uniformly ridiculed any suggestion that the sisters were involved in proselytizing. One older, olive skinned girl with dark hair and black eyes commented: "Some of the nuns obviously don't like Jews and make no effort to hide their feelings. With others it's hard to tell. But none try to sell their religion." A blond boy pointed out that at the insistence of the sisters before each meal Jewish blessings were offered and Jewish religious songs were sung. "First time I heard these." His tone suggested that he would not be unhappy to do without them.

That evening, after our first exposure to what proved to be an unending sequence of what many of us considered almost inedible meals, I sought out the girl who had defused some of the worry about religious indoctrination. While I had been relieved by what she had said about the nuns, I wanted to know about the camp and the people running it. She turned out to be very direct and not at all averse to talking about herself and about the camp. We told each other almost immediately that both our fathers had been arrested and sent to Dachau. Hertha was almost exactly my age, and we soon found out that we had many things in common. She was one of the few girls that I knew who played chess better than I did. Like me, she loved to read and she was very interested in politics, left wing politics. We quickly became good friends. Once I tried to kiss her, but she turned me away, saying that love was bourgeois and not for young Zionists and Socialists like herself.

The camp, according to Hertha, was not too bad. The main problems were that food was not exactly what most of us had been used to, and there were not enough books to read. But otherwise things were pretty good. Work was certainly not onerous, although some of the children were chronic complainers. The park was lovely and we could roam over it at will. There was an area where we could plant vegetables, even a green house. To leave the park, however, we had to obtain permission from one of the sisters.

"Except to go to school. If you go outside the park at any other time, the gatekeeper will surely report you. He and his sons are Nazis. Unfortunately there are quite a few of them even in Holland. He'll try to make trouble for you with Sister Monika. Luckily she doesn't pay too much attention to him."

"Sister Monika, she is the one in charge, right? When she stood on that chair I expected her to start issuing marching orders. What's with her? I hope she doesn't fancy herself as the commanding general!" I added: "Boy, in her talk she didn't waste one extra word. I bet she is one of the nuns who doesn't like Jews."

Hertha did not agree. "If she dislikes us, she does not show it. She seems to treat everybody the same. She strikes me as being quite fair. But I know what you mean about her martial demeanor. Perhaps she learned that in Spain. I heard she spent a year there as a nurse in a military hospital. And man, can she be tough. One of the girls one day did not show up for her morning kitchen duties. Just stayed in her bed, next to mine. Apparently she decided that six in the morning, was too early for her."

Hertha shook her head as if to question how anyone could behave like that. "No excuse, either. Sister Monika came into the room to see what was going on. At first, she talked rather quietly, telling the girl that it was only fair that each of us did their share of the work. The girl just lay in her bed without responding, and stared at the Sister almost insolently. Boy, it really shocked me. Monika then tore into her, raising her voice almost threateningly, telling the brat that she would not tolerate such anti-social behavior among the children in her charge. I guess she has quite a temper. The loud voice scared the girl. She started to cry, but got up, put on her clothes and went on to do her work." Various versions of the girl's treatment and the Sister's anger quickly made the rounds of the camp.

1939: Sister Emmetta.

So, I thought, our Sister had spent time in Spain. As a Catholic nun that would have been with Franco's fascist troops! To me that was almost as much of a sin as being a Nazi. What business did she have being in charge of a camp of Jewish refugee children? In spite of Hertha's comments, she must hate Jews. That's probably why she was so hard on that poor girl. A Fascist in charge of the camp. I was appalled and enraged. What could I do? Nothing. I had the same feeling of helplessness that I experienced when the children's train was showered with rocks in Frankfurt.

The next day Sister Emmetta called us together and told us about our work schedule. One week on, one week off. One group of children for breakfast, one for lunch and dinner. Others to wash clothes, clean the rooms, set tables, wash dishes, serve food. It did not sound very difficult to me and I was surprised when a few of the children raised objections once more. Again it was mostly the religious boys who complained, who felt that such work was only for girls. Emmetta had obviously heard all this before.

"Sister Monika is in charge here and she has said that it is only fair that everybody does his or her share. I know that she feels strongly about this. Those of you who think that you cannot abide by her dictum will have to speak with her." This settled the matter. Not one of the boys had the temerity to confront the formidable Monika. Clearly, most of us agreed with her decision, but I felt offended by the authoritarian manner of passing down the word of the seigneur.

Because of my age, I was among the group that first had the early morning shift. Our work was quite easy. Under the direction of one of the sisters, we heated up a brew loosely referred to as tea: brown, sweet and of unknown origin. It came in large, garbage can-like containers. Stale sandwiches came in large boxes. These we unpacked, transferred to metal serving trays and then distributed them on the big dining hall tables. Occasionally we also heated a cereal, a porridge, whose taste was easily confused with that of library paste. After breakfast we washed the dishes and food containers and cleaned up the dining hall.

The next few weeks passed rapidly. I got to know Sister Emmetta quite well. She took her job very seriously; wanting to be fair to all the children, assuring that the older ones did most of the hard work, yet assigning some tasks to all over ten. Her worried look hardly ever disappeared. She was patient with all the children, and never raised her voice. Perhaps because I was one of the oldest children in the camp, she frequently asked me questions: Was the work too hard? Were the children unhappy? Why was so little of the food eaten? I don't think that my answers were very informative. While I made friends with three or four children of my age, I did not interact with most of the others. I was not religious, so I did not participate in prayer sessions.

We saw little of Sister Monika. She gave Emmetta a free hand with the organization of the work. At least two of the Sisters were openly anti-Semitic. One suggested that the problems we were facing was retribution for our having killed Christ. The other said repeatedly that there were poor, hungry Dutch children, so 'why feed rich Jews?' I noticed that whenever Sister Monika was nearby, this type of talk disappeared quickly. There was no question that she was in charge and that none of the other nuns wanted a confrontation with her. And whatever her feelings about us might have been, she maintained an appearance of absolute fairness.

As we soon found out, many people from The Hague visited the large park. On Sundays and holidays they came on their bicycles from all parts of the city. The ponds had not only white swans but also many multicolored ducks swimming on them, In spring and summer they and the many flowers and blooming shrubs added to the feeling of festivity. Families came with their children. These often flew gaily-colored balloons or kites. On the rare days when the sun shone, the park took on a particularly joyful air. On these days I frequently experienced jealousy and resented that others should be able to enjoy such pleasures, and felt acutely the absence and threatened permanent loss of my own family.

Among the park's multitude of trees and bushes, the most spectacular were the many groups of Rhododendrons. These were arranged so that each cluster formed a dense, green ring around a space in the center. In the late spring and early summer the Rhododendrons were in bloom. Then these made gigantic red, pink or white circles. We soon discoverer that the bushes served a non-decorative purpose as well. Frequently two bikes, one a man's the other a woman's, were parked near one of clusters. Many of us received our first graphic sexual education by very quietly observing the goings on in the hearts of these clumps.

Late in January the winter became cold. There was now ice on the paths and the ponds froze over. Some of the grass turned a nasty brown. Outside the park was a canal, one of Holland's many. It too froze over and became an avenue for many ice skaters. Sister Emmetta asked several of the older children if they were skaters. Four of us, all boys, knew how to skate. The sister managed to round up skates for us and on a Saturday afternoon we went with her on an excursion. We skated on the canal for about three or four miles. It was easy with the wind pushing us along. Not so on the return trip. Now the freezing wind was in our face, slowing us down and making every mile seem like an endurance run. The sister did not seem to be affected by the wind nor aware of the problems we were having. She skated ahead of us, waiting every few minutes to allow us to catch up to her. When we finally returned to the camp, Emmetta arranged for us to get a cup of hot 'tea', and then the four of us collapsed on our beds. I don't think I even bothered to have supper.

The next Saturday Emmetta invited us to go skating again. This time only three of us accepted. We went for a longer distance, following a canal that was new to us. Skating with the strong wind pushing us along would have been a pleasure, had we not worried about the return trip, unnecessarily so as it turned out. We stopped skating near a streetcar stop. "It will take us close to our camp". Sister Emmetta, who had paid our fares, was in a talkative mood. Occasionally she even smiled. She told us her age, twenty five, and that she came from a town several miles north of The Hague.

"There are very few Catholics there", she added for reasons not obvious to me then.

Sister Monika and she were the first nuns at the camp and had to make the arrangements necessary to house fifty children. "You are lucky to have Sister Monika. She works very hard for you and is very conscientious."

We asked more about Sister Monika. "We had a difficult time forgiving her", was Emmetta's first comment. "Forgive her for what?" we wanted to know. Emmetta's frowns made her suddenly look older than her years. The conversation had obviously taken a turn that she did not relish. "Perhaps I should not talk about this. But I thought that everybody knew".

"Knew what?"

"Her year in Spain; How could she work with the Godless Reds? But now she has returned to us." Emmetta clearly wanted to end that conversation. The other boys didn't seem to care, but I was completely astonished.

53

"I am going to go fight with the Godless Reds if I can. At least they are against the god damn Nazis."

The sister looked at me almost in horror. Then she relaxed: "You are not even thirteen years old. You don't understand. And don't use such language. I don't think your Jewish god would like you to use his name in vain."

So I had been totally wrong about Sister Monika. It must have taken both courage and conviction for a Catholic nun to oppose the obvious preferences of the hierarchy. I felt quite foolish and at the same time relieved and puzzled. Why did she return to her order? The news from Spain made it obvious that any type of help was badly needed by the Republican side.

On Sundays I had been going to a local Rabbi to prepare for my Bar-Mitzwa. On the last day of January I was to be thirteen years old, to become a man according to Jewish tradition. The rabbi was a modern Jew, a Zionist, interested in the events of the world, a very sympathetic man and a good host. His wife always provided me with something to eat: cookies, sandwiches or even a piece of cake. I had started to question whether I went to their house for the Torah, or the food. After the conversation with sister Emmetta I decided not to go again. My Jewish God did not seem to pay much attention to the fate of his flock. Why should I pay attention to his teachings?

My birthday coincided with that of the venerated Dutch queen, Wilhelmina. It was also the last day of a morning kitchen shift for me. I could not get myself to get up at six in the morning. Time passed, almost seven, and I still lay day dreaming in my bed. Not unexpectedly, Sister Monika strode into the room. "Why are you not in the kitchen?" Her tone was anything but friendly.

"Not today" I lamely stammered.

"What's special about today?"

"It's my birthday"

It took several seconds for the sister's face to soften. Then she smiled: "Well, you are not our queen so you better be prepared to go to work tomorrow to make up for today." With that she strode out in her usual manner.

"Boy, you are lucky, that the old battle-ax did nor eat you alive." The boy in the bed next to mine had been awakened by the encounter.

That evening there was a celebration of the Queen's birthday. We were served a special dinner and several of the women from the refugee committee attended. To my amazement, some of them brought me birthday presents. Little trinkets, to be sure, but presents nevertheless. The old battle-ax evidently had telephoned them; how else would they have known?

About the middle of February, Sister Emmetta arranged for another skating excursion. This time she was rather secretive about our goal, but she did say that it would be a longer trip and that we would return by train. The same three skaters that had gone on the last journey went again. Because of the length of the trip, we had to leave by ten in the morning. I skipped school, one of the few Saturdays that I did so. We skated for several hours before we came to a small town.

"We can have lunch here" the Sister told us. As we walked into the village with our skates tied over one shoulder, Emmetta purposely led the way. It was obvious that she knew exactly where she was headed.

"I grew up near here", she said to no one in particular. At a small shop, it looked closed to me, she knocked at the door. The man who opened it greeted Emmetta with obvious affection. She said a few words to him and he, speaking in good German, invited us into his shop.

He and Emmetta started to speak in rapid Dutch. I could only make out a few words. Emmetta was asking about her parents, particularly about her father. Apparently she had not heard from them in a long time. Then I heard even less because a woman, perhaps the man's wife, brought us a plate full of sandwiches and glasses of milk .The three of us needed little encouragement to dig in. The sandwiches were on fresh bread with cheese, jam or chocolate. Wonderful.

It was soon time to go to the train. The storeowner refused payment for the food, and Emmetta paid for our tickets. We had a third class compartment to ourselves. In the whole car there were not more than two or three other people. As the jerky motion of the engine started to accelerate the train, Emmetta began to cry. It seemed as if each lurch induced more tears. The three of us were quiet, not knowing what to do or say. As the train's motion smoothed out, her crying subsided. Her face maintained a despondent, almost tragic quality. She looked at us in a questioning way, perhaps debating with herself whether to tell us the reason for her despair.

"I was born near here," she almost repeated herself. "My parents and three brothers live on a farm about two miles from the village. I haven't seen any of them in four years." She started to sob again.

It seemed to take great self-control on her part to continue. "Father is a strict Calvinist. Religion is very important to him. When I became a Catholic, he was furious. After I entered the order, he told me never to return and forbade my family from having any contact with me. They all obey him." She was silent again, for several minutes. "I don't know what I would have done without Sister Monika." She was quiet for the remainder of the trip.

1939: Sister Monika.

It seemed to me that the running of the camp improved with time. Or was it my realization that Sister Monika was not a fascist? It may also have been the weather. The ice began to melt in late February. Rain came frequently, but there were days of occasional glorious sunshine. Sister Monika seemed to lose much of her military demeanor, and she smiled more frequently. She not only knew the names of all the children, but also much about each child's specific problems. While she still brooked no nonsense, most of the children appreciated her fairness and concern for each of us.

One evening, I had just finished an after dinner kitchen shift, Monika stopped me as I was about to go to my room. To my surprise she said to me:

"If you want some hot chocolate, why don't you come to my room? I'll make us some. "

We went to her small bedroom. There she had an electric plate. She heated some milk, then added sugar and a piece of dark chocolate. Two cups were filled with the hot liquid that tasted very good on the cold, damp, evening.

"Tomorrow, when you wake up, I will no longer be here," she said suddenly and without warning. "I have been told to go back to my order. I should not have hit that girl." One of the older girls, a red haired, chronic grumbler, had complained once too often. About the food, her room mates, the unfair treatment she received from the Sisters or God knows what. When Sister Monika could not calm her verbally, and the laments became more irrational, the nurse had boxed her ears. It couldn't have been very hard, because the blow left no mark. But now the girl had something real to complain about and wasted no time. She spoke to as many of the committee members as would listen to her, telling them all about her horrible mistreatment.

The result was the removal of Sister Monika. She was ordered not to tell any of the children about the events until the day of her departure.

"I lose my temper too easily; that is not what God wants. What will I do without you children?" When I did not reply, because I was really stunned, she went on: "I am not telling you this for my sake, but I may not be able to talk to you again. I have heard that you want to go to Spain. You know that I have been there. Other boys your age have done it, so I know it's possible. I understand why you want to go there. But don't do it. It is too late. That war is lost and in any case it isn't what you think. Not now. At least it isn't what I thought. A few years ago it might have been. Now the Russians call the tune and it isn't ..." She did not go on to tell me what it was not.

Now I was doubly stunned. That she should leave the camp was a terrible blow. To me she had represented continuity in the uncertain new world in which I found myself. Other Sisters came and went, but Sister Monika remained. I had begun to greatly admire her fairness and concern, as well as her occasional necessary toughness. Perhaps I needed an adult to revere. I had started to idealize and idolize Sister Monika. The prospect of her leaving hit me like a personal betrayal. Why did she have to slap that stupid girl? Perhaps she should have apologized. And how could she say those ridiculous things about Spain? Not only did I then not understand what she meant in her comments, but also I was absolutely sure that, whatever she meant, she was wrong. To me that battle was black and white. The evil fascists against the noble Spanish people. What was wrong with the Russians calling the tune? They seemed to be the only ones that had the strength and the will to stand up to the Nazis.

Not until years later, when I read Orwell's "Homage to Catalonia", did I realize the terrible betrayal that she must have felt when the Stalinists brutally eliminated all opposition within the Republican ranks and thereby sealed the doom of the Spanish democracy not only then, but for many years to come. When she went to Spain to help the Republican cause, she surely believed that this offered a clear way to fight the black fascist evil that was overtaking Europe. Then she had found the same horrible darkness on her side as well.

Tears of frustration and anger came to my face. I felt as though I was being abandoned. Sister Monika put her hand on mine. When I tried to withdraw it, she held on tightly.

"Don't think that I don't know how you feel. Once I almost lost faith in my God." She emphasized the my. "Perhaps in a few years you will understand what I am trying to tell you." She had been talking to me like an adult, but I was crying like a child. I tore myself away from her and went to my room. I lay on my bed crying and sobbing for some time until I could regain control over my emotions. The next morning Sister Monika was gone and I never saw her again.

A few days later I happened to over hear a conversation between two women, both members of the committee. It was in rapid Dutch and I could only make out part of the conversation.

I gathered that there had been a strong disagreement within the committee about what to do about the charges made by the girl. The two of them had defended Sister Monika against efforts by several other members who wanted to have her fired immediately. Others, while appreciating her qualities, were afraid that the neo-Nazi press might have a field day if a scandal developed. Finally, all agreed to leave the decision to the superiors in Sister Monika's order. This was clever politics. The committee could point to the religious hierarchy as being responsible for the adequacy and fairness of any steps taken to insure the proper operation of the children's camps. I could not make out if the two women approved of this shifting of the onus, but they at least went along with it. I think the decision of the committee was without dissent. So it was her own superiors, acting almost surely only after consulting the local Catholic power structure, which insured that Sister Monika would be removed from her position. It is difficult to believe that her being on the "wrong" side in Spain was not at least partially responsible for this decision.

April 1939: Baseball.

I had almost given up hope of ever seeing my parents again. After six months in concentration camps, Father's chances of surviving much longer seemed slim. Mother was still in Vienna, trying desperately to get him released, my sister in England where she had gone on a transport very similar to the one that had brought me to Holland. The British were not as afraid of offending the Germans as the Dutch; presumably they thought the channel provided sufficient protection. She had been "adopted" by an English family, who had sent her to a boarding school, just as they would have done if she had been their own child.

Within their financial and political constraints, the Dutch committee and staff made the daily life in our camp as pleasant as the circumstances permitted. All but the smallest of the children could attend Dutch public schools, but attendance was not compulsory. The school attended by the older children was about 20 minutes from the park, a walk none of us minded. On Saturdays, the Jewish day of rest, almost all the children stayed in the camp. Another boy, he was about thirteen, and I were the only ones who went regularly, even on Saturdays. I enjoyed going back to school. I even learned to speak Dutch reasonably well. Languages came easily to me, and I was interested in participating in the day to day class activities. Another reason why I liked school was that most of the teachers leaned over backwards to treat us with kindness and sympathy, quite a contrast from our last Viennese experience. The Dutch children did make fun of our attempts to speak their language, but otherwise they took their cue from the teachers. We had no serious problems with any of them.

I had come to accept the likelihood that events would force me to stay in Holland by myself for a long time. So I took my schooling seriously. Speaking Dutch might become a necessity. Today, it may be hard to believe that a 13-year-old would seriously consider the dark alternatives of his future in such a way, but Jewish children grew up very quickly in the days preceding the holocaust.

After school we did our homework, played chess or other games, wrote letters or worked on small green garden plots where we planted lettuce and other vegetables. When we were able to harvest these, they supplemented our monotonous diets. Mail was passed out once a day and this was an important event. Letters were the only connection to the past and constituted a direct assurance that the writer, usually a parent or sibling, was unharmed and still cared. We older children quickly became adjusted to our work routines and performed our daily chores. The work was not hard and only a few objected to doing their share. Aside of the assigned tasks, we had a lot of freedom, at least within the confines of the camp, and quickly learned to become self-reliant.

For many of us making daily decisions, even about such small matters as what clothes to wear that day, or whether to go to school, was a new and heady experience. I did not find it unpleasant.

Our biggest complaint was about the quality of our food. Our meals were made up of the extra fare not required by the patients of a city public hospital. Breakfast and lunch consisted of stale, open- faced sandwiches that frequently were several days old. These were almost invariably smeared with peanut butter, or with jam; occasionally some were covered with cheese or with margarine or sprinkled with small pieces of chocolate. The peanut butter was frequently rancid; it had acquired a pungent odor, and tasted dreadful. To this day I find that smelling even fresh peanut butter tends to make me gag. The chocolate covered sandwiches also acquired an odd odor when too old, but the strong flavor of the chocolate allowed them to remain edible.

Our dinners consisted of a mixture of boiled potatoes and a vegetable: sometimes spinach or chard, sometimes carrots or turnips. At other times it was impossible to tell what the vegetable was before it had been boiled and became irreversibly mixed with the soft, overcooked potatoes. The consistency of this unappetizing mixture invariably resembled that of watery mush. It all tasted the same and we distinguished it only by its color: green mush or red mush. Once a week, on Saturdays, dinner included a piece of fat, boiled beef, while on Sundays our hosts gave us a hard-boiled egg. This we regarded as a special treat.

I want to emphasize that we were not being starved. There was no reason to be hungry, there was always enough to eat. Yet we were rarely full. But this was our own choice. In view of the extreme starvation that most of these children very likely later faced, before their terrifying, ultimate fate, even to voice these grievances today seems outrageous. Many of us, however, came from middle class Jewish families. As far as food was concerned, we were spoiled, used to eating well. Probably none of us had ever encountered a steady diet of thoroughly unappetizing meals.

On the rare days when the weather permitted it, we played ball games on the large lawn just outside our building. There I learned to play baseball. Because of the almost daily rains, our field was frequently muddy. It was not exactly level. Right field sloped gently, or in parts not so gently, away from the rest of the green, making catches in the outfield doubly difficult. The batter's box was at the highest point of the field. As a result, home runs in this park were not exactly a rarity. None of this bothered us,, many of us played enthusiastically and with great intensity and winning each game seemed very important.

In April of 1939, I don't remember the exact date, Sister Emmetta interrupted such a baseball game. She wore her usual serious worried expression. When I first met her, I had often wondered what events in her life had caused such sadness. After our skating trip to her village I assumed that it was the relationship with her family that weighed so heavily on her small shoulders. When something truly pleased her, a rare event, a smile would appear out of nowhere and she seemed to become a different person.

On that day in April, I was playing outfield in the sloping right field. The Sister came across the grassy expanse and called me as she came towards me. She had what looked like a telegram in her hand. It almost surely meant one of two things. Father was either dead or else he had, miraculously been released from the camps. Because of my innate pessimism, or perhaps out of self-defense, I had conditioned myself to accepting the former.

As the Sister approached me, my first strange thought was: "Why did this have to happen during a baseball game?" Emmetta, her most worried look on her face, handed me the unopened telegram and stayed close to me as I tore off the brown cover. She was not unaware of its likely, sad content.

What stared me in the face, however, was: "Dad returned safely from trip. Letter follows. Mutti."

I let out a yell: "My Father got out of Buchenwald."

Members of both baseball teams started to scream and to run towards me. A boy my age, but much smaller, a very religious Jew with whom I had very little in common and very little contact, ran to me from third base where he had been waiting for a chance to make the uphill run to home plate. He jumped on me and put his arms around my neck. Because of the sloping terrain we both fell over, I backwards. The other players reached us and formed a circle with the three of us in the center. The Sister, now smiling and her face almost angelic, helped us up and then put her arms around both of us. The children were yelling, shaking my hand, clapping me on the back. Fathers, and even one mother, of five or six other children had also been arrested and sent to the camps. Mine was the only one released, but surely their hope now was that others would soon follow.

The Sister turned to me: "If you want to send a return, I'll gladly pay for it." The Sisters had very little money of their own, yet most of them were always willing to help. I did want to answer, but could only think of: "Congratulations. Hope to see you soon".

My newly found optimism that I would soon see my parents was not totally unfounded. In her last letter to me, Mother had written that all four of us had obtained visas to go to the Dominican Republic. I found out later that my aunt in Romania had bribed a Dominican consular official in Bucharest to approve and speed up the necessary documents. The Dominican dictator, Trujillo, looked with favor on the immigration of whites to his 'republic'. He despised his neighbors, the black Haitians, with whom the Dominicans share the island of Hispaniola, and he wanted to enhance the whiteness of his own people. For this reason, after payment of the appropriate 'mordida', emigration to the island was not quite as difficult as to other parts of the world. My aunt had also offered to pay for, or perhaps she had already bought, tickets for the boat trip. Very likely these extremely generous acts were the catalysts responsible for Father's release and probably saved all our lives.

Within four weeks after the first telegram, I received a second. This one was not from Vienna, but from Antwerp, Belgium, only a few miles from The Hague. It was also short: "Arrived here happily. Will make arrangements for you to join us soon. Plan to stay here at least for the near future. Mutti and Papa".

The Belgians had given my parents transit visas so that they could board a ship leaving Antwerp for the Dominican Republic. My parents had no desire to go there, but would have done so only as a last resort. Father and Mother made sure that by the time they arrived in Belgium the ship had already departed. They then consulted a lawyer who filed the necessary papers that allowed them to stay in Belgium while the authorities debated their case. Refugees quickly lost their individualities and their fates determined in files manipulated by bureaucrats whose primary interest frequently was the retention of their jobs.

August 1939: Island.

Events hardly bore out my parents' and my rosy view that their children soon would be able to join them. What happened in the ensuing months was a minor, perhaps typical demonstration of the insanity of the times. The Belgians would not grant an entry visa to either my sister or me, not even a twenty-four- hour visitors' permit so that we could at least see each other. Neither the Dutch nor the British allowed my parents to visit either one of us. This in spite of guaranties by the Dutch and British committees that my parents would not overstay their visa duration in either country or, alternatively, that the children would not remain in Belgium.

Letters were written back and forth, many government agencies from all three countries became involved, but to no avail. Perhaps my parents did not push with sufficient vigor. Their existence in Belgium was clearly precarious and they could not afford to offend the already reluctant host country. They lived in a tiny one-room apartment on Rue Bien Etre, the Street of Well Being.

After Father's experience in the camps, in ten months he had lost one third of his body weight and two of his toes were frozen and had to be amputated, life in Belgium seemed like a paradisiacal existence. I think he would have willingly stayed in Antwerp as long as he was permitted to do so. He did not want to jeopardize his new lease on life. Belgium, he thought, would remain out of the war, and Europe would sooner or later return to its senses. He was willing to wait, not to upset the status quo. Mother also realized that their position in Belgium hardly was the most secure and that they needed to behave with circumspection. She, however, did not expect times in Europe to get better within the foreseeable future and she was afraid that sooner or later Belgium would fall victim to German expansionism. Hence she was the one who pushed to pursue all leads that would place an ocean between the Nazis and us.

After two or three months of letter writing to exalted officials of three countries, signing of many petitions, and receipt of many refusals, all concerned seemed to accept that in the political climate of the times nothing could be done to enable parents and children to see each other.

I told myself that I was not really that anxious to see my parents nor to return to them and be under their strict control. Father had grown up on a farm outside Vienna. His father, like most Austrian farmers of that time, was a strict disciplinarian who saw no reason to allow any of his children even a little freedom. A generation later, Father's view had only moderated slightly.

There was, however, one woman on the Dutch committee who felt that governments may be bound by absurd rules, but people were not. She was an enthusiastic and dedicated Socialist, and I had confided to her my romantic desire to go to Spain and fight for the Republican cause. She had children of her own that were only slightly younger than I was, so she was particularly sensitive to the situation that had overtaken us. Not that our situation was unique. A few hours' train or boat ride separated many parents from their children, but national laws and international fears prevented them from spending even an occasional few hours with each other.

This woman, whose name I have now forgotten, it is much easier for me to remember faces, came to visit me one Saturday afternoon. It was raining intermittently, hardly unusual weather for a Dutch summer, and I had been soaked by a downpour that caught me on my way from school. She said without going into any detail:

"I have made arrangements for you to see your parents. I have also talked to Sister Monika before she left and she agreed. You are to come with me tomorrow. I will pick you up at six in the morning. Be sure to be ready; we have a long way to go."

She was in a rush and I did not question her about where we were going or how this meeting had suddenly become possible. My mind became occupied with other things, trivialities. The question of clean clothes suddenly became important to me. Normally it did not matter to me if I wore my underclothes for a week at a time. Now I nearly panicked when I realized that all my underpants were in the communal laundry and not due to be returned for another two days. A friend, who was about my size, loaned me a pair; he was astonished at my sudden concern with cleanliness.

A look in the mirror told me that my hair resembled a bird's nest; I probably had not combed it in days and I badly needed a haircut. Permission to take a shower on days other than Tuesdays and Fridays had to be obtained from one of the Sisters. The one I asked was totally astonished at my request. When I coupled that with a wish to get a haircut, she thought that perhaps I had undergone a religious conversion. On hearing why I was behaving in such an

68

unheard of manner, she gave me a few coins of her own money and told me to go to the barbershop, some ten minutes away. Again the incredible generosity.

"Just before going to bed, you can take a shower. No sense doing it now, you'll just get yourself dirty again."

After the haircut another crisis arose. My two pairs of shoes were an indescribable mess, caked with thick, hardened, brown mud. There was no shoe-cleaning material in the camp. I was afraid of what Father would say if he saw their state. They had very likely not been cleaned since I had left Vienna. I took one pair and went into the bathroom and turned the faucet on full blast. The shoes went under the stream of cold water. The sink took on an ugly shade of brown as more and more of the stubborn mud dissolved. Finally, the water became clear. Not only the outside of the shoes had become wet, but their interior as well. I put them on the next morning. They were then still soaking wet. I did not mind; at least the shoes looked reasonably presentable.

At about nine o'clock, after making sure that I had a complete set of clean clothes, I took my shower and went to bed, but did not get much sleep. Usually, I slept like the proverbial log, but that night I woke up several times to look at the big clock that hung in the room that I shared with five or six other boys. Each time I awoke it became more difficult to go back to sleep, and I began to realize that perhaps my parents meant a lot more to me than my mind had been willing to acknowledge.

It turned light around five in the morning. I was wide awake by then and quickly got up, washed my face, and put on the clothes I had laid out for myself the night before. Everything was clean. Water from my shoes formed little puddles on the floor after I stretched them so that I could force the unwilling leather over my feet. I looked at the clock: ten minutes after five. Six o'clock seemed like an eternity away. I did not want to wake up everybody else in the room, so I tried to read. My book lay on the box in front of my bed. Each bed had a box like it. It was used both as nightstand and storage for our clothes. Although I had enjoyed my book the day before, now I could not get my eyes and brain coordinated. My eyes jumped from word to word and line to line but nothing seemed to register in my memory. After I had spent ten to fifteen minutes of fruitless attempts at digesting the content of one page, Sister Emmetta came into the room.

She smiled when she saw that I was already dressed.

"I came to make sure that you would not be late for your ride. I see I need not have worried. If you want a cup of hot tea before you leave, come to the kitchen."

I did want something hot. In the kitchen one of the other children gave me a cup of the brown liquid. As I drank it, I was in the unusual position of sitting down while others were fixing the day's breakfast.

Now it was almost six and Emmetta and I went outside. A few minutes after six the Vauxhall sedan drove up. Two women sat in front. The driver was the committeewoman I had befriended; the other, who opened the backdoor for me, I did not recognize. It was still very dark.

Stretched out on the back seat was a little girl, perhaps five years old. I had to squeeze into a corner so as not to wake her.

"That's Erna, she is from Berlin. She is also going to see her parents," one of the ladies said quietly.

After many miles, the girl next to me woke up. "Where are we?" she asked sleepily.

"And where are we going?" I added somewhat less sleepily, although the night's lack of sleep, the emotional stress and the smooth vibrations of the car had made me drowsy.

"We are near a town called Hoek Van Holland," one of the women answered, speaking slowly and carefully. "There we will leave the car. Then we go on a boat. The boat will take us to an island that is close to Belgium. If everything goes according to plan, your parents will also come to that island. You will have most of the day to visit with them. In the evening they will return to Belgium, and you will come back with us to The Hague."

Clearly the simple words were directed primarily at Erna. I have no trouble remembering her name; Erna was also Mother's twin sister's name.

"I'm going to see mummy and daddy," the little girl started to yell, and "I'm going to see daddy and mummy." This was repeated with one intonation and then another for quite a few minutes. "But why can't I go with them in the evening? I don't want to come back with you." Quickly her happy mood had changed to despair and she started crying.

"If you children want something to eat, there is a bag of sandwiches and some chocolate on the shelf above your seat." The driver had experience in diverting the mind of a five-year-old away from painful to more acceptable subjects. "But eat the sandwiches first and only then the chocolate. "

The girl stopped crying almost instantly, reached for the bag and started to eat one of the sandwiches. After a very short while she pushed it aside and went to work on one of the chocolate bars. No one stopped her. I nibbled on one of the sandwiches. Although it contained cheese and meat, and tasted just fine, I could only eat a few bites. I wrapped the rest in the paper in which it came, and stuck it in my pocket. There it stayed until the next day when I ate it with great pleasure. I asked Erna if she had any bothers or sisters. She had none.

We had now been driving for perhaps two hours. I occasionally worried about the day's events. Would our parents come at all? What could I say to mine, particularly to Father? Had he fully recovered from the damage inflicted on him in the concentration camps? Surely he would think that after his experiences anything I might say would be trivial. I was also confused about my feelings towards Mother. Living by myself, or at least away from my parents, had certainly changed me. Had my absence equally changed her? Or perhaps had her worries about Father so depleted her emotional reservoir that she was no longer able to include me? I remembered painfully the times in Vienna when she had barely been able to function. Had she recovered? I was afraid that the Psalmists might be right and that "Father and Mother have forsaken me".

It was easier not to think about such things. I looked out my window. There were only a few cars on the road. The flatness of the Dutch country side was interrupted by many well kept farm structures, actively turning windmills, and occasional clumps of leafy, very green trees. In contrast to present day car travel, when high-speed highways assiduously avoid almost all populated areas, our route then passed through many small villages. These were distinguished primarily by the steep church spires that pierced the gray sky, towering over all other man made structures and even over the trees. There was a sameness and almost dreariness to the landscape that matched the grayness of the sky. Only occasionally was there a break in the cloud cover that had accompanied us ever since we left The Hague. Then, sunshine would appear briefly, and the greenness of the fields, the colors of the often freshly painted houses, the glistening of the wet trees and the wet shining steeples of the churches would suddenly and strikingly change the appearance of the country side. I was fascinated by these sudden, short-lived transformations and delighted by the contrasts that they provided.

We arrived in Hoek Van Holland after what seemed like an interminably long trip. Near one of the boat terminals there was a parking area. We were early; the first boat was not to leave for another forty minutes. We walked around the harbor. Neither Erna nor I had ever seen ocean-going vessels. Most of the ships in Hoek van Holland, according to the adults, were ferryboats. These went to England, Germany and even as far away as Norway. I was thinking how wonderful it must be to have papers that permitted one to go on board here and exit in another country without the harrowing travail of obtaining visas.

We finally boarded a small boat that was to take us to the island. Most of its passengers apparently were vacationers; the island was a popular resort. People went there for day trips, but also for longer periods. Many brought their bicycles along. The holiday spirit was unmistakable. Family groups, young adults or students and many couples all had that anticipatory look that vacationers seem to take on. As the boat left the dock, almost exactly at nine o'clock, many of the young people cheered loudly.

The boat trip took less than an hour, but it was the longest boat ride that Erna and I had ever experienced. The two women found seats in the main cabin. They and Erna stayed there for the entire trip.

I went out on deck, but not until I had been told to be careful because: "Your parents would prefer see you dry rather than dripping wet."

The sky was still gray. Occasionally a few drops of rain fell. In the distance, on the ocean, I could frequently see patches of sunlight reflected from the white waves. I stood on the stern and watched the bubbling foam that developed near the ship's propellers. Then I walked to the bow and observed the boat bouncing through the oncoming waves. There was enough wind so that the boat yawed and pitched noticeably. I fantasized that the boat was sinking and that I had drowned. How would my parents react? Mother would surely cry, and that pleased me a lot. Of Father's reaction I was less sure. He too would grieve over me, but I did not think that he would cry. In reality, the weather was rather mild for the North Sea, and at no time were we even in the remotest danger of having an accident.

By the time the boat entered the island's harbor, I had gone back into the cabin. The two women were talking animatedly, and Erna was nodding while holding the last chocolate bar in her hand. The conversation, in rapid Dutch, was about Germany, whether war would break out, and if Jews should leave Europe. Even in countries not yet overrun by the Nazis, some Jews were acutely aware of the dangers facing them. Unfortunately, only a very few were willing to act. As I heard them sat, to leave one's home, job, friends and family for an uncertain existence in a strange country was not a decision easily made. As a result, most Jews stayed behind until it was too late to leave.

The boat had now been sitting in the harbor for some time. All the other passengers and their bicycles were gone. Still the conversation continued and the women made no move to leave the boat. I was becoming very impatient and my fidgeting was finally noticed by one of the conversationalists.

"We have to wait for the harbor master to come and take us to his home. It will only take a few minutes," one of the women said.

She then told us what the arrangements were. Not only Dutch, but also Belgian boats brought visitors to the island. Our parents would be on one that was due to arrive in a few minutes. Legally they were not permitted to leave the boat, since they had no entrance visas that would allow them to step on Dutch soil. If however, it was suspected that they might commit some crime, the Dutch authorities could arrest them, keep them on the Island until departure of the ship and then insure that they would leave again. The harbor master, who was the highest civilian official on the island and also an old Socialist comrade of one of the women, had agreed to arrest the two sets of parents, take them on land and keep them for the day. But instead of taking them to jail, he had generously offered to make his own home available for the day. Furthermore, he would not report the arrest to his superiors, so that no record would appear that could later adversely affect either set of parents.

"The whole thing sounds insane, when I describe it," she had turned back to her companion and switched to Dutch. "But this is Europe in 1939. You can't imagine the things I tried to arrange this meeting, before an acquaintance suggested this. When he first described what we would have to do, I thought that he had been reading too much Kafka". I had read recently read Kafka's 'The Trial', so I knew what she meant.

The harbormaster soon came. He was a small man, about my height, with a face that one might have expected from someone constantly in touch with the sea. His complexion was ruddy, and his nose almost bright red. A small cap covered the remnants of his blond hair. I would guess that he was about fifty, but could have been anywhere between forty and sixty. An attractive smile turned almost into a grin as he came over and shook hands with the women and with me. After a few words of welcome, in Dutch and then in German, he picked up the little girl, who oddly enough did not at all object, and carried her out of the cabin, over the gangplank, and onto the dock. We followed him and Erna up a hill to a house that overlooked the harbor. He was no longer carrying her, and she was now walking next to him and engaged in what appeared to be a serious conversation, obviously in German. I was always astounded at the language abilities of so many Dutch people.

The front door to the house was open, and as we came close, a woman wearing a traditional Dutch apron over her dress came out. She waved at the man, obviously her husband, and immediately put her arms around the little girl. With the girl in her left arm, she then came over to shake hands with the rest of us. She kept her free hand on my shoulder as she talked in strange Dutch that at first I could not understand. From the few words that managed to sound like the Dutch I had learned in school, I gathered that she was welcoming us and telling the women that we could have use of her house for as long as we wanted. There was much other conversation that I did not understand at all.

We drifted into the house. After passing through a small antechamber full of foul weather gear, umbrellas, coats and oilcloth pants, we came into the living room. I can't recall much about it, except that there were photographs of people, perhaps family members, everywhere. The furniture was simple and comfortable. We sat down on the chairs and sofas, Erna on the lap of the harbormaster's wife. He himself had not come in with the rest of the group.

Suddenly Erna jumped off the woman's lap, and nearly flew to the open door. I had to turn around to see what had aroused that sudden activity. The harbormaster and four adults were approaching the house. I also jumped up, raced outside and nearly knocked down my parents. Mother grabbed me first. She kissed me and I kissed her. Then Father put his arms around me. I don't remember that he ever kissed me before, but he hugged and kissed me that day and I hugged and kissed him. There were tears in his eyes, something that I never witnessed before. Mother cried openly.

We probably said the usual trivial things to each other as we walked to the house, but I am not sure. Perhaps we were all silent. Father, as we entered the house, told the harbormaster that we could never thank him enough for what he was doing. The Dutchman's smile again turned to a grin. In the house, introductions were made, hands were shaken, and expressions of good will and thanks were on everybody's lips. Then the harbormaster's wife took Erna and her parents into the bedroom. The other adults somehow disappeared from the living room and I was left alone with my parents.

Now I had my first chance to look at them. Mother really did not look very different from when I had last seen her in Vienna. Her face looked more relaxed, her cheeks were flushed with the excitement of the reunion, and perhaps she had gained back some of the weight that she had lost after Father's arrest. The big change was in Father. He looked at least ten years older than I remembered. His weight must have been many pounds below what it had been before his arrest. Formerly a heavyset man, he now looked almost thin. When I commented on this, Mother simply said:

"You should have seen him three months ago".

His face was actually tanned; he and Mother went for long daily walks in Antwerp. Occasionally his eyes took on a vacant stare that almost frightened me. Later, when Mother and I were alone for a few minutes, she told me that when he first returned from the camp, this stare was almost always present. Now it happened only rarely, when he was particularly excited about something. Father walked with a marked limp, the result of his loss of two toes, but he insisted that he was doing better every day, and Mother agreed.

We now talked non-stop. About my sister, other relatives, about friends, my parents' own life and about plans for the future. For the first time I heard that there was an excellent chance that we might soon get visas to go to the United States. Only a few weeks ago Mother had mentioned in a letter that this was a remote possibility. My parents also brought out food for our lunch: cold Wiener Schnitzel, pieces of fried chicken, hard boiled eggs, fresh bread and even some fruit. As the day progressed, I kept eating more and more without really being aware that my parents were hardly eating at all. They asked me detailed questions about my daily life, school, did I have friends, and, several times, did I get enough to eat. As I wolfed down more and more of the victuals that were to be lunch for the three of us, they seemed to find it more and more difficult to believe that I was fed adequately. Father really surprised me; he took great interest in my answers and frequently asked questions. In Vienna, where he was always occupied with business matters, he and I only very rarely had real conversations. Mother, who usually dominated family talks, was unusually quiet. She frequently put her hand on mine, and kept handing me more food and urged me to eat. It was obvious that she, too, was surprised at Father's interaction with me and was content to listen.

The day slipped by. At three o'clock the harbormaster's wife came into the room. The Belgian boat was to leave in half an hour. She then went into the bedroom to deliver the same message to Erna's family, then came out again, waved at us and left us alone again. Mother cleaned up the remnants of the meal and suggested that I take with me what little food was still uneaten. By this time I was so full that I refused. My parents exchanged an odd look. Only then did I realize that I had consumed not only my lunch, but most of theirs as well. Some months later, when we were on the ship going to New York, my parents told me that they thought I must have been starving in Holland. As a consequence, they had done everything possible to speed our departure from Europe. In this curious fashion, my hunger for good food might have saved all our lives. Only four months after our arrival in the U.S., the Germans invaded Holland and Belgium and all escape routes became shut.

Suddenly there was a loud wail from the bedroom. Erna had just realized that her parents were about to leave. She was inconsolable, yelling that she wanted to go to Belgium with them, that she hated her parents, that she was going to jump off the ship and swim to Belgium, and that she never wanted to see her parents again. Soon the crying mother carried her screaming daughter from the bedroom, while her father came behind, carrying various bags and looking totally miserable. Mother walked to the girl and said something to her that I did not hear; it had no effect. We all tried to distract the girl. Nothing worked. She also had eaten more than her share, so that food no longer had any allure and could not be used as a bribe.

It was time for the parents to depart. Although the boat going back to Holland was not to leave for another forty-five minutes, the harbormaster insisted that we part at his house. He did not want any children to come to the Belgian boat. Children accompanying the "arrested" parents might have looked suspicious. If there was a Belgian Nazi among the passengers, who might have realized what was going on and complained to the Dutch authorities. That might have caused trouble for the harbormaster and surely would have stopped him from ever doing anything of this nature again. So his wife took the child, who was now screaming hysterically, from her still crying mother and into the house. My parents and I kissed several times, then somewhat formally shook hands. Father's final comment to me, he couldn't resist asserting his parental authority, was:

"Don't forget to thank the two ladies for arranging this"

When I returned to the house, Erna had stopped her screaming. She was lying on the sofa with her head in the lap of the master's wife. The girl was sobbing quietly now, while the woman was talking to her in a melodious, soothing voice. She was obviously used to dealing with children. Indeed, I now noticed that the family photographs all showed children.

A few minutes later Erna fell asleep. The two women from the refugee committee, who had disappeared for the entire day, now returned. Dutifully I thanked them both for myself and my parents. Whatever I said surely wasn't enough. Without their special efforts and kindness this reunion would not have taken place. After the war, when I returned to Holland in an American uniform, I attempted to locate several of the committee members. Among those the Dutch police reported as 'resettled in Poland', the euphemism for having been sent to the extermination camps, was my benefactress. Erna and her family almost surely were also swallowed in the blaze that rapidly engulfed the European Jews.

i

September 1939: Visas.

Even before the Germans marched into Austria, my parents' business, importing radios from various European countries and the parts needed to repair these, became less and less profitable. In the late thirties the Austrian economy, like that of much of the rest of Europe, was in shambles. To attempt to increase sales, my parents hired several traveling salesmen. Austrians like fancy titles, so these were called business representatives. The titles did not, however, increase their rather meager income. These men scoured Vienna and the Austrian countryside, trying to persuade owners of retail stores to handle the radios that my parents imported.

Several of these salesmen became my parents' friends. Father was a generous man, and except for those who were put off by his occasional explosive temperamental outbursts, employees stayed with him for years. Some of the salesmen were Jews, others not. They all occasionally came to dinner at our apartment in the suburbs of Vienna, so I got to know several of them. One in particular, a man who called himself Joachim Kleiner, his true name was Isidor Kleinfeldt, came quite frequently and became a good friend of the family. When he married, in 1937, we all went to his wedding.

When the Germans arrived in Austria, Father, although he was well aware of the treatment that German Jews were then receiving, was not too worried about his own fate or ours. My paternal family consisted of farmers that had lived in Austria for several centuries. They always considered themselves more Austrian than Jewish. Father would not or could not believe that the German State would not regard him similarly.

Mr. Kleiner's outlook was not nearly as confident. At the end of World War I, his family had followed the retreat of the Austrian army from Poland to avoid the anti-Jewish excesses occurring there. The Kleinfeldts had settled in Vienna only to feel acutely the Austrian anti-Semitism that found its most severe expression against Jews from Eastern Europe. Isidor was not a name that would attract business, and Kleiner sounded much more Austrian than the obviously Jewish Kleinfeldt.

Name changes did not impress the Nazis. The Nuremberg racial laws required proof of 'non-Jewishness'. A true Aryan was one who could prove that each of his four grandparents had been baptized. Sadly, the German churches, perhaps unwittingly, cooperated with this policy by issuing the necessary certificates of Baptism. Had they refused to do so, the racial laws could not have been enforced. Kleiner knew very well that his name change had only a minor cosmetic effect. He was convinced that Jews had no future under the ruthlessly efficient Germans. He and Father argued frequently over the need to provide a safe escape, but Father was convinced that the patriotism of his family members, their long tenure as farmers, and his own service as an officer in the Austrian cavalry during World War I would deflect from us most of the anti-Jewish edicts that he, too, thought were coming.

Only two weeks after the enforced marriage of Austria to its violent and insistent suitor, Kleiner approached Father. Business was already at a near standstill; only a few loyal customers were still willing to buy from a Jewish merchant.

"I received a letter from a distant cousin of mine in Cleveland, in America. He wants me to come there. He writes that I need to be quick, and register as a visa applicant at the American Embassy. Why don't you come with me and register your family?"

American immigration law then was based strictly on quotas. Congress set limits to the number of natives from any one country that could emigrate to the US. annually. The size of the quota varied from country to country. For Britons and Northern Europeans it was large, for Germans and Austrians and East Europeans smaller, and for Chinese and Japanese effectively zero. Kleiner's cousin had pointed out that early registration for a visa application was essential, or the quota could rapidly become over-subscribed.

"You just go and register yourself," Father told him. "I'm not interested. It's none of my affair. I don't plan to emigrate."

Kleiner was persistent. "What do you have to lose? Come with me. Even if you never go to America, registering doesn't cost anything."

But Father was not interested. "Just take the day off, and do what you need to do. There's no work to be done here in any case."

"Well, perhaps I can register both of us at the same time. Why don't you give me the vital statistics of your family?" This Father did, perhaps as much to stop the conversation and get Kleiner out of his hair as for any other reason.

The next day the salesman came to work as usual. "You were smart not to come with me. There were hundreds of people at the Embassy. I had to stand in line for over four hours before I even reached the Embassy doors." Just one month later he might have had to stand for twenty-four hours. By then the Austrian quota was filled not just for 1938, but for the next several years.

Kleiner added almost as an afterthought: "But now my wife and I are registered and so is your family."

Father did not attach much significance to that conversation, and almost forgot that it ever took place; I don't know if he ever informed Mother. After Father's imprisonment Mother did not actively pursue emigration to the US. It was too much of a long shot and if Father was to be released form the camps, he needed a host country willing to take him immediately.

To be allowed to settle in the United States was not a simple matter. An American resident had to testify, in the form of an affidavit, that the immigrant would not become a burden to the US government. This affidavit was so important it took on a mythical character and European Jews talked about it as if it came from the Torah. Mother was well aware that verifying an affidavit and the subsequent bureaucratic activity could take months and that that was more time than Father might have.

The only person we knew who lived in the U.S. and who might be willing to give us an affidavit was Father's cousin. Fritz had lived in Berlin, but visited Vienna periodically; his parents and most of his other relatives lived in Austria. Everybody in our family was extremely fond of him. He had a wonderful, deep, sonorous laugh that reflected his sunny interior. In 1935, he decided it was time to get out of Germany. He was then working as a furrier for a well-known Berlin salon. Fortunately for Fritz, his boss, also a Jew, had come to the same conclusion. He had had the foresight to move most of his money to Switzerland and the United States and so was able to move his business to New York. He asked Fritz to join him. In those early days of Nazi power, such things were still possible. Fritz readily accepted. He, his wife, and their young daughter crossed the ocean and settled in New York City.

When Fritz heard about Father's arrest, he immediately wrote that he would see what he could do about providing an affidavit. This was easier written than done. To the US immigration officials, financial responsibility meant that your bank account showed a balance of at least ten thousand dollars, quite a sum at a time when the annual salary of people like Fritz did not exceed three to four thousand dollars. By scraping together all his savings, he could only muster a little more than one thousand. But he was not one to give up easily. Several of his Jewish friends and business associates were in similar situations. They also had relatives in Europe whom they wanted to help, but their financial position was no better than that of Father's cousin.

So they concocted a very simple but effective scheme. By pooling their resources, they could assemble a total of well over ten thousand dollars. Every penny that they collectively possessed went into one single account and was recorded in the name of one member of the group. He was then able to give an affidavit to his relative and the immigration people could satisfy themselves as to his financial status. No sooner were the papers sent to the appropriate American Embassy, than the money was withdrawn from that account, put into a different bank under the name of the next affidavit writer. The scheme may not have been legal; Fritz never asked. It saved the lives of many people, including those of our family, and that was enough for him.

After Father's release from Buchenwald, in June of 1939, when my parents had reached Belgium, they were notified by the American Embassy in Brussels of the arrival of this fabled affidavit and that it had been verified as fulfilling immigration requirements. But the letter that contained this good news was actually very discouraging. It informed them that, since they were only now registering for emigration to America, the earliest date that a visa was likely to be issued was 1947. The Austrian quota was filled until then. The letter went on to say that, upon payment of a few francs, the Embassy would immediately initiate an investigation to determine whether our family 'met the moral and legal eligibility requirements for emigration to the United States of America'. In addition to payment of the fee, my parents were asked to supply all our family's vital records, where we had lived in Vienna and 'any other information that you might think pertinent to your case. Make sure your current address is correct and include your phone number, if any.'

This bit of bureaucratic mumbo jumbo was not really a surprise, but it nevertheless had a depressing effect on my parents. Father was willing to stop right there. By 1947, he felt quite rightly, the Nazis would surely be overthrown or defeated in the war that everybody knew was about to break out, or, "we will all be dead". Mother had a different perspective. While she agreed with the political reality of Father's view, she though that having the affidavit and the family's eligibility on record could not cause any harm and might just possibly have beneficial consequences. They had been able to go to Belgium on the strength of a visa to the Dominican Republic. Perhaps other countries would accept them temporarily if they could demonstrate that their ultimate goal was America and that it was only a matter of time before they would reach that permanent haven.

It cost only a few francs to let the investigation proceed, so Father saw no point in getting into a prolonged argument. He was well aware that in the long run he would give in anyway. So the necessary information was sent to the American Embassy, but my parents continued their search for havens elsewhere. They were in contact with friends in Argentina and in Australia and they filled out pages and pages of applications at various consulates and embassies looking for avenues to escape from Europe. Months went by without any positive responses from anywhere. The letters to various friends and relatives became more desperate. My parents renewed their visas to the Dominican Republic and started to make inquiries about conditions in the capital, Santo Domingo. The political situation in Europe deteriorated further. The gullible Chamberlain went to Munich and returned to London proclaiming "peace in our time" as he betrayed Czechoslovakia to the increasingly rapacious Nazis. Mother began to worry acutely about their safety in Antwerp. The Belgian Nazis became cockier week by week, exerting pressures on the government to restrict movements of Jewish refugees. To its credit, the ruling Conservative Party successfully resisted these.

During all this, my parents' day to day existence remained quite pleasant. Father's health improved rapidly; in spite of the two amputated toes he could now walk easily and they went for ever longer daily strolls. They made friends with a couple that had operated a famous art gallery in Vienna. This friendship became a life-long one, spanning three continents and many years.

Although my parents' one room flat was tiny and they had to watch expenditures very carefully, they managed adequately on the money made available to them each week by a Belgian refugee committee. Were it not for the volatile political situation in Belgium and in the rest of Europe, and their inability, in spite of many attempts to do so, to have their children join them, they might have become quite content with their life. As it was, they felt under continually increasing tension.

Early in June, my parents received a phone call from Holland regarding the meeting that had been set up on the Dutch island. This happened on a Sunday, a week before the reunion was to take place. My parents did not have their own phone; there was a pay phone in the ground floor of their apartment house. The chubby Flemish concierge who was responsible for the management of the apartments usually answered incoming calls. Any long distance call was rare, but a call from a foreign country, even from Holland, was a real event.

On the following Monday they went for their usual walk. When they returned, the concierge was very excited. She said in her far from fluent French: "You had another long distance call." She looked at my parents with considerable respect. "Two long distance calls in two days! This one was from Brussels. The man spoke with a foreign accent. Perhaps he is a German. Here is his number. You should ask for Edvard." My parents had no idea who the mysterious German named Edvard might be.

Making a long distance call from a pay phone was then a complicated business. Tokens, obtainable at a nearby tobacco store, had to be placed in a slot. After the connection was made, and frequently that required several attempts, the tokens were swallowed up by the machine at a frightening rate. If the slot ever became empty, the connection was interrupted without warning. Mother went to get enough tokens to complete even a long conversation. She returned to find the concierge still talking with Father. The woman made no move to leave, obviously wanting to satisfy her curiosity about all these long distance calls.

It took a few minutes to get though to Brussels.

"Ambassade Americaine". Father was totally surprised and did not respond immediately. "Ambassade Americaine, American Embassy", the voice now sounded slightly irritated.

Father now answered in his best commercial English. "I was told to speak to Edward."

"We have a Mr. Edward in immigration. Do you want to speak to him?"

"Yes, Mr. Edward, please."

"Ne quittez pas," the operator reverted to French. After an interval that ate up several tokens, Mr. Edward came to the phone. Father introduced himself and said that he had been told to call. Mr. Edward was quiet for a while, perhaps looking for the correct file on his desk.

"Ah, yes. Here it is. We have completed our investigation and it appears that you and your family are eligible for emigration to the United States. You will, however, have to wait your turn. The Austrian quota is filled for at least three years, probably more like six. There is also one complication and that is why I thought that I should call you." Complications were almost never good, and Father waited for the bad news. "The Foreign Service Officer in Vienna who handled your case," all refugees became cases, "sent me a note that there is a family Hahn registered with the American embassy in Vienna. To him and to me it sounds very much like your family. What is going on? Is this the same family, or isn't it?"

Father was about to deny such a possibility, when his memory suddenly produced the name Kleiner. It appeared out of nowhere. Hadn't the salesman offered to register us? Perhaps he really had. And now the Americans might think that Father was doing something underhanded. He was an honest man; dissembling was difficult for him, and the conversation had totally taken him by surprise. He could not weigh the pros and cons of denying or admitting the possibility. He finally simply told the truth that he just did not know whether Mr. Kleiner…"spell that name, please," who had offered to do so had actually registered us or not. Father could only say that it certainly was possible.

Mr. Edward was an understanding man. "Odd things happen in this crazy time. If it is really the same family, and we will have to check this thoroughly, your quota number, based on the date of your Viennese registration, will be reached within a month. The Embassy can then issue you a visa immediately. Be sure that you have valid passports for all four of you. Good…"

In the excitement, Father had forgotten to feed the hungry telephone more tokens and it retaliated by cutting off the conversation.

English was not Mother's forte. She had not understood any part of the conversation, which Father now reported in rapid German. The Flemish woman, who understood neither German nor English, was beginning to think that something devious was going on. One thing she knew: she did not like Germans. Father finally turned to her and said in French: "It was a man from the American Embassy, not a German, who called. He had good news for us."

The woman went into her apartment hoping that the foreigners who received long distance calls were telling her the truth. But they must be important; why else would Americans call them, and from Brussels! But then why did they live in such a small apartment?

Several days later my parents took the early morning train to Brussels. They only had to wait two hours at the American Embassy before Mr. Edward could see them. He was a young man, not yet as cynical as most other Embassy officials. Father's ability to speak English made things easier. The man was surprisingly friendly.

"I have checked with my Viennese counterpart and verified that a Mr. Joachim Kleiner and his wife had registered the same day as the date of your registration. All the other details that you gave me were consistent, I am convinced that the Belgian and Viennese Hahn families are indeed one and the same."

After checking with his superior, he told my parents that as soon as they brought their passports, they could have their visas. They would be dated October 1 and could be used for a period of one year.

"You know, I have to give bad news to so many people these days, it really is a pleasure to be the bearer of good news." He actually said something like: "I am happy for you." Curiously, he then asked Father how long it would be before there was a war in Europe. At least one year, Father thought.

He was quite wrong. Within two months the Germans and Russians had signed a non-aggression pact and then invaded Poland and divided it among themselves. France and England declared war on Germany, and the period of the "phony war" started, a time when the Allied and German armies remained within their well-fortified positions without making any effort to engage in active combat.

Our ship was not to leave until December. We could only hope that passage would still be possible then. We were in luck. Early in December, the four of us left for New York on the Dutch liner SS Staatendam. The ship returned to Rotterdam just as the phony war came to an explosive end with the German invasion of Belgium and Holland. The ship was sunk when the German Stuka dive-bombers ruthlessly attacked and crushed that city and its harbor. Crushed were also the hopes of all but a few of the remaining European Jews to escape what not much later became the final solution.

December 1939: Liberty.

In October of 1939 our passports were stamped with the all powerful American immigration visas. Immediately our lives were transformed. While we had not become handsome princes, our status as ordinary human beings seemed to have been restored. The Belgians no longer considered my sister and me pariahs whose presence could endanger the stability of their state. Almost magically, transit visas appeared on our passports, and first I and then my sister rapidly joined our parents in Antwerp. I went there by train. It was an uneventful trip about which I remember nothing at all. My parents met me at the train station. Of that re-union I recall much less than about the meeting on the Dutch island. I did notice immediately that Father's walk had improved. His limp now was almost imperceptible. He had also regained some of his former weight.

Curiously, while I can picture my parents' appearance at the time, even the dress Mother wore, I remember almost nothing about their reaction to me or my reaction to them. I am certain that Mother was excited beyond words. Only a few months earlier she had faced the possibility of never seeing her husband or her children again. And here was the realty that within a day the family would be reunited. Father must have been equally thrilled. But I remember nothing. Perhaps the events of the last few months had drained my emotions to the point where I could no longer react even to an event as important as reunification of my family.

The first night in Antwerp I slept in my parents' small room on the second floor of a modest apartment building. In one corner of the room was a small counter with a sink and a hot plate, the kitchen. In another corner was a closet; when I opened it I found a wash basin and the toilet. A room with a bathtub was down the hall and was used by all the tenants on that floor.

My parents had accumulated all kinds of good things to eat, at a considerable financial sacrifice, I am sure. But I was not particularly hungry. We talked until quite late in the evening. I found out that a date had been set for our departure to New York, six weeks away in early December. We were to leave from Rotterdam on a Dutch liner, the 'Staatendam'. I was again told that Mother's aunt in Romania had loaned or given us the money for the tickets.

The next day, I think it was a Sunday, Lucie arrived from London. My parents' room was not big enough to sleep four, so they rented another small room on the fourth floor of the same building for the two of us. The two small beds it contained occupied nearly the entire room leaving just enough space for a chest of drawers and a washbasin. The toilet was two doors away in the hall.

I had not looked forward to sharing a room with my sister. In Vienna, to my parents' consternation, we had quarreled ad nauseam. I objected most to her nagging about my clothes. My leather pants were too dirty; my socks not neatly pulled up below my knees, my shirt and suspenders were crooked. This seemed to be a daily litany. In retaliation, I did things like embarrass her by reading aloud from her diary during one of her birthday parties. To the surprise of both of us, in Antwerp, and for that matter for the rest of our lives, we got along famously. Perhaps it was the year's separation; perhaps the rapid maturing that had been forced on both of us.

The first few days in Antwerp were wonderful. My parents showed us around the handsome city. The enormous harbor and the many ships loading and unloading cargo from every conceivable place in the world particularly impressed me. The size of the ships far exceeded that of the puny boats I had seen in Hoek van Holland. Food was plentiful and tasty. But above all we were so glad to be together that we ignored any minor conflicts that may have arisen.

Unfortunately, this happy situation did not last too long. Father had always been a stickler about table manners. In Vienna our table was set with white linen and our maid served the meal. Now we sat around a small table, covered with an oilcloth that had seen better days. Dishes and glassware were shabby, reflecting our current economic situation. We served ourselves. But Father had to demonstrate his authority by maintaining strict table protocol. All food on my plate had to be eaten. While in Vienna this had caused me to spend many hours staring at fish that I hated or rhubarb that I detested, now this was no longer a problem. I happily ate every scrap of food at each meal. But other things surfaced to make meals more of an ordeal than the pleasure that they were the first few days in Belgium.

"Don't talk with your mouth full of food".

" Don't have your elbow on the table while eating."

"Sit up straight. Only peasants eat the way you do."

"Don't make so much noise while chewing your food."

"Keep your elbows off the table."

This went on at every meal; at first it was said rather pleasantly, but when it became obvious that I was not too anxious to follow all his commands, Father's voice became louder and he added words like: "how many times do I have to tell you these things". Finally he resorted to: "You are not all that stupid." The familial meals lost their appeal and became battles of wills that I could not possibly win.

"At the end of each course, when you are finished, put your knife and fork across the plate, the knife towards the center of the table with its edge inwards. I really get sick and tired of telling you the same things over and over again."

This time I was not able to keep quiet. "When you were at Dachau, I am sure your table manners were really helpful, right?"

Father's reaction was immediate. He reached across the table to slap my face. I recoiled instinctively, so that only the tips of his fingers touched my face, His face was purple with anger.

"How dare you talk to me like that? Who do you think you are?"

It was surely an arrogant and insensitive question, but I suppose nothing unusual for a teenager. The fury of Father's response reflected the frustration he must have felt at his inability to be in absolute charge of our relationship as he had been in Vienna. Sadly, never did I have the feeling that he had any understanding of the changes that I had undergone in the eighteen months of our separation. Even sadder was the inability of either of us to discuss our worsening relationship. It was almost a cliché: the father- son confrontation. In our case it was accentuated by his experiences in the camps and by my recent freedom from parental supervision.

In Vienna he had been the respected owner of a business employing 20-25 people. Not only had he lost all this, but also for several months he had to endure indescribable horrors and indignities. Little wonder he tried to establish at least one immutable point in society as undisputed head of his immediate family. He needed respect and thought it my duty as his child to obey him unquestioningly. As a teenager I was only concerned with myself. I could not understand or sympathize with his unenviable and, as it turned out untenable, position.

I was far too concerned with establishing my own new standing within my family. It seemed to me that both in Vienna and in Holland I had demonstrated that I could survive even without my parents. Hence, in my view, I was no longer to be treated as a child.

These two diametrically opposed views set the stage that soured our interactions for the rest of our lives.

Mother also tried to reconstruct the relationship she and I had in Vienna before the arrival of the Germans. Sometimes her attempts were almost comic. "Wear a sweater, it's cold." "Carry an umbrella, it might rain," and even "be careful when you cross the street". But I could laugh at these. It was easy for me to talk to her. When I pointed out to her that in Holland I had been able to handle my day to day affairs even in her absence, she simply said:

"I know that some of these requests must sound silly to you. I often think about Vienna and the happy times we had. Then I think of you and Lucie as you were then: children. I am so happy to have you back, that it is sometimes difficult for me to remember how changed you really are."

I had no trouble understanding what she meant. After our conversation, however, her admonitions became much less frequent.

She was practicing to make leather flowers, so she would have a salable skill in the US. These flowers were intended to be worn much like custom jewelry. I don't know who sold her on this idea, but she had neither manual dexterity nor a good sense of visual esthetics. As a result, her flowers were amateurish in execution and unattractive in design. But she continued producing more and more. Perhaps she thought that practice would make her into an artist.

My sister did not have the problems with my father that I encountered. Lucie was older, and perhaps that made some difference. Certainly she was more adaptable and less the rebel. She rarely opposed Father and he in turn hardly ever raised his voice when talking to her. In the evenings, when we were by ourselves, she would complain about him, object to his seeming stubbornness and tell me that Father was too hard on me. She managed, however, to avoid direct confrontations.

As the time to leave for the States became close, we all agreed that we should try to speak only English. Neither Mother nor I knew more than a few words. Both Father and my sister proved to be good teachers. We all tried our best to abide by this decision, but obviously this limited conversations severely. Mother had the most difficulties. Curiously, in those days whenever she gave up on English she tended to revert not to German, but to French.

The morning we were to board our ship we took a train to Rotterdam. From the train station we splurged on a taxi that took us to the port. The Staatendam was a large passenger ship of the Holland-America line. It seemed to me to be enormous, a good deal larger than even the boats we had seen in Antwerp. Its shinning white paint advertised its interior cleanliness and sense of order and with it a relief from the uncertainties of the last eighteen months.

After our papers were carefully checked, both by police and by officials of the Steamship Company, we were allowed on board. A steward took us to our third class cabin. He was courteous and friendly. The cabin was small, perhaps eight by six feet, but well organized, with two sets of two layer bunks that could be folded against the wall, a small table, room for our baggage, and of course a toilet and shower. There was not a spot of dirt anywhere and the chrome fixtures were polished brightly.

That evening we sat down to our first meal on board. The dining room tables were set with white tablecloths, linen napkins, and shiny settings. Our cabin number identified our table. A waiter brought us menus. Quite a contrast to the way we had been living the last few months.

All the tables were full. The conversation all around us was almost exclusively in German. Apparently most of the passengers in third class were also Jewish refugees escaping the Nazi inferno. We, however, continued to speak English or at least Father and my sister did. The first meal consisted primarily of freshly made sandwiches filled with meats and cheeses that I had never tasted before, with a pudding for desert. It all seemed like a fairy tale.

Before going to our cabin, we sat down in the passenger lounge. The first evening drinks were free. My sister and I were introduced to a strange and, at first taste, unappetizing liquid called Coca-Cola. Mother joined Father, who was drinking a beer, by having a glass of wine. This she did only very rarely, perhaps once or twice a year. It accentuated the importance of the event.

"It's to celebrate our last day in Europe." This she said in French. German had become the lingua non grata.

"Do you think we'll ever go back?" I think it was my sister who asked the obvious question.

I should not have been surprised at the vehemence of Father's answer: "As long as the Nazis are in power I would have to be dragged back. I would rather starve in the US than come within a thousand miles of those swine."

Yet, as the conversation went on, it became obvious that both my parents were sad about having to cross the ocean and worried about their future. They talked about the nice times that we had had in Vienna, the summers at lakes in the Alps, the occasional trips to Italy. Life in a world that for us no longer existed. We knew little about what to expect in the States. Letters we had received in the last few months stressed how difficult it was to find jobs even in the land of milk and honey. We were all concerned about our future. My own vision of the US was mixed. According to Mother, I was supposed to have been named after a US Supreme Court judge, Louis Brandeis, whom she greatly admired. How Louis in my case ended up as George is a tale I have long ago forgotten. My hero from early childhood on was Abraham Lincoln. These positive aspects of my feelings about the US were contaminated by Communist propaganda about exploitation of workers and economic hardship of the poor. American capitalism was not to the liking of a thirteen year old Socialist.

It was difficult for me to follow the French and I fell asleep in my comfortable chair. It must have been after ten when my sister woke me up. She and I went to our cabin while my parents continued their melancholy conversation.

The next morning I was up early, before seven. Everybody else in our cabin was still in bed, so I went on deck. We had left dock during the night and were now out on the open sea. The sky seemed pitch dark, but the ship was brightly lit. The war may have been in its phony phase, but it was wartime nevertheless. Two spotlights brightly illuminated the Dutch flag. Anyone approaching, even a submarine, would readily see that this was a ship from a neutral country.

It was cold and the moist, icy wind made walking uncomfortable. Hardly any passengers were on the third class deck, even on the sheltered side of the ship. I wandered around for at least half an hour and then returned to our cabin. By then the rest of the family was up and dressed.

At breakfast Mother was beginning to feel ill from the ship's motion. All she wanted to eat was a grapefruit. She didn't know the English word so she asked the waiter in French for "une pamplemousse." This he brought, but forgot to include a spoon. I went after him and, in Dutch, asked him to bring one. He looked at me in surprise; I suppose that not too many passengers could speak his mother tongue. From then on whenever he saw me he would smile and greet me in Dutch.

The weather was getting worse. In December the North Sea is frequently rough and it certainly was so during our crossing. Even the big liner was tossed about by the strong wind. Mother did not take kindly even to the grapefruit. After eating it, she became violently seasick and had to go to the cabin. For the rest of the voyage she did not leave her bunk for more than a few hours.

It took Father a little longer until his intestines also responded to the rolling and pitching motion that seemed to intensify as the day wore on. He also found it necessary to spend most of his time near the bathroom of the cabin. Most other adult passenger seemed to have been similarly afflicted.

Neither my sister nor I had any feelings of nausea. Many other children also were spared the feared mal de mer. In the absence of parental control, we were free to roam over much of the ship, play whatever games we wanted to play. We behaved as if we belonged to a flock of birds that had suddenly been released from captivity.

Our sense of liberty was most evident at mealtime. Of course we had no financial worries, since food was included in the price of tickets. There was no one to remind us to watch our manners. Frequently now there were no more than half a dozen adults in the large dining room that accommodated perhaps one hundred people. The waiters were not at all busy, and frequently our waiter would have no one to attend to except my sister and me. He had a good sense of humor, joked with my sister in English and with me in Dutch. Best of all, he brought us whatever food we wanted.

"More Chicken for Madame? Another steak for you, Sir? Right away!" He always was excessively polite, addressing us formally but smiling at the same time. And ice cream! It was my first introduction to the American version- silky smooth, I thought and what wonderful flavors! Best thing I ever ate, it seemed to me.

"Why don't you try peach, Sir? Or Strawberry? I could also bring you a piece of cake from the first class kitchen .Not many of the rich people are eating."

I had both. Cake and ice cream. Pure heaven.

Towards the end of the voyage the weather improved. Mother still spent most of her time in the cabin, but Father joined us for meals. Seemingly he and I could not help ourselves. Our battles started again. As we approached the Statue of Liberty I had the distinct feeling that the time of my liberty was coming to an end.

January 1940: New York.

We stayed in New York only about six weeks. There we lived with distant relatives of Father's in an area called Washington Heights. It is now mainly black and Puerto Rican, but in the late thirties it was a favorite of Jewish refugees from Germany and Austria. German was almost a second language; many of the stores had signs in English and German. German sausages, Austrian bakery goods and Jewish newspapers were sold everywhere. The area was quiet, and in many ways reflected the taste of the recent immigrants. It seems to me that there were many small cafes and restaurants, bookstores, and movie houses that showed European imports. Even cars drove slowly, perhaps because some of the streets were curvy. It was almost as if the refugees had been able to recreate the mood and pace of a central European neighborhood.

Elsewhere in New York, however, the excitement and ferment of the city was impossible to escape. Everything, I thought, existed in superlatives. The skyscrapers, the many, many cars, and even the people seemed bigger than their equivalents across the Atlantic. Cars and people moved at dizzying speed. My senses could not readily adjust to the volume of noise in the streets. After dark, and dark came early in the winter, I found the many flashing lights disorienting. The first time I was in the subway during rush hours I had a vision of what hell must be like. At the same time the electrifying energy that permeated the metropolis exercised its effect on me. I was alternately wildly excited or suffered from a freezing emotional numbness.

We were desperately poor. After two weeks in the States, our entire monetary supply had shrunk to not much more than about $100. Father could not find a job. This was the tail end of the great depression. Work was difficult to obtain even for young Americans. Not surprisingly, no one seemed to want a forty-five year old immigrant whose English was limited, who had no knowledge of the American scene, and who had no demonstrably salable skills. Prospective employers were not impressed by his degree from the Austrian Academy of Commerce. Nevertheless, Father answered many employment ads that appeared in the papers, followed up every lead that relatives and acquaintances offered, all to no avail. I don't know how he managed, but he showed no outward sign of discouragement. Every morning he went traveling to various parts of the city to look for work. Frequently, in spite of his amputated toes, he walked many miles to save the subway fare, then a nickel.

Mother made more and more of the leather flowers. She became somewhat more adept at producing arrays of these in various colors and combinations. While her dexterity improved somewhat, so that the ornaments did not look quite so amateurish, her creative abilities did not keep pace. I found her products quite unattractive. She mounted the flowers on cardboard, perhaps twenty bouquets per display. Father would then take these and attempt to sell them to the stores in our neighborhood. But when he found that few if any were storekeepers were willing to buy the flowers, he left them on consignment. This also proved unsuccessful. Most customers apparently shared my evaluation of their lack of attractiveness.

Our main meal was now in the evening. This was not so much to adjust to American custom, but for practical reasons. At noon, Father would frequently be away from the Washington Heights area. My sister and I had started school; it was easier for us to take a sandwich and not to have to return to our rooms for lunch.

The conversation at dinner now was primarily about money. I still had to contend with frequent admonitions about my table manners. But these, at least temporarily, were overshadowed by financial worries.

"How long can we last at our present rate of spending?" Father would ask.

It was Mother who handled the bookkeeping, a euphemistic term in this case, because all she could enter was red ink.

"You know as well as I that my flowers are not selling. If things don't improve, in a month, two at best, we will be totally out of money." Not that this needed repeating. We were all aware of the problem. At times some of the comments made by my parents sounded as if we were about to starve. Actually the problem was not quite as acute as all that. Organizations existed that provided food and pocket money to needy German and Austrian refugees. Furthermore we were staying with relatives who had made it amply clear that even if we could not pay our rent, they would not toss us out into the street. Father, however, was determined not to accept gifts from others. In Belgium he had had no choice; his state of health needed time to recover. Furthermore there was no legal way that he could accept work. The terms of the Belgian transit visa strictly forbade gainful employment and the authorities made sure that this rule was obeyed. In the US, however, his attitude was that we were here to stay and that it was up to him to find a way to provide for his family.

One evening after the usual conversation about impending financial disaster, Mother said to Lucie and me: "Children you need to do your part. Why don't you take a selection of my flowers to school and see if your teachers want to buy some?" She thought that anyone would be pleased to wear her creations. Mother never seemed to doubt her aesthetic abilities, even in the face of commercial failure. I was amazed at her ability to mix hardheaded realism with a naive romanticism that at times approached self-delusion. My sister and I looked at each other. I knew Lucie felt about Mother's flowers the same way that I did. But how could we object? The daily conversations about money had made it amply clear to us that any source of income had to be pursued. So we agreed. The next day both of us took one of Mother's displays with us. She to high school and I to elementary.

I had no idea how I was going to approach my or any other teacher. Certainly not in front of the other students. I had rolled up the cardboard on which the flowers were mounted and then wrapped the tube with newspaper so that other students could not see what I was carrying. Ridicule from them would have been too much. So I waited until the end of the school day and stayed in the classroom until all the other students had left. Then I mustered all my courage and showed the teacher the display of flowers. Father had put prices on each flower group. This made it obvious that I was attempting to sell them. The woman looked at the flowers and then at me, I thought I detected a look of pity. My face must have reddened. I felt as though I was begging, and indeed so it may well have seemed to her.

Perhaps she was used to dealing with penniless refugees. She smiled at me, picked out two of the flowers, paid for them, and said something like "These are really very nice-did you make them?" Her comment hardly helped. Did she think the flowers so amateurish, perhaps childish? Even more discomforted, I mumbled something about Mother having made them. The teacher must have been a very sensitive person. She immediately realized that her comment had made her evaluation of the quality of the flowers obvious.

She turned to me. "Tomorrow, at lunch, I could take these and show them to other teachers. I am sure they would also like to buy some of them. If you will trust me with the display."

Trust her? I would have gladly given it to her. The next day, after class, she returned the remaining flowers and gave me money for those sold. Five dollars? or more? I can't remember. I felt ashamed to take the money and even more ashamed to be glad to get it.

The pressures of the last few months took their toll. In class occasionally I started to cry without any obvious reason. When the teacher asked me why I was crying, I invented sad stories. My friend had been killed in a concentration camp; a relative had died; my sister's boyfriend had disappeared. After the first few stories the teacher no longer asked me. She obviously no longer believed me. I hated to cry in class, but I could not stop myself.

It was again in the evening, at dinner, that Father suddenly asked how we would feel about leaving New York for good.

"Where would we go?" was my question.

"How would we pay for our trip?" Lucie asked.

"One thing at a time." Father said. "As you know, there is a refugee committee with offices not far from here. They have counselors that try to help refugees find work. I have been talking with some of them about our situation. All of them realize that it is next to impossible to find work in New York. They are trying to disperse us throughout the country."

Mother interrupted him. "I think some of the counselors, and more importantly, some of the donors that supply the agencies' funds are afraid that too many refugees, Jewish refugees, in any one place would cause a backlash against local Jews. Anti-Semitism, unfortunately is not confined to Europe."

She allowed Father to proceed. "When I said that I would like to get away from New York, as far as possible, California was the obvious choice. There are already many refugees in Los Angeles and in San Francisco. So those cities are out. The place they suggested is Sacramento. I know very little about it, but it is probably as good as any. As far as money is concerned, they will lend us the bus fare."

Although he was asking us how we felt about moving, it was clear after a few more minutes of conversation, that my parents had already discussed the matter and decided to go. So Lucie and I were just being asked to concur. I felt very ambiguous about the project. Certainly I did not enjoy our pressured and insecure existence in New York. On the other hand a new move meant more uncertainty, and I was almost desperate for some continuity. It would also mean the fourth new school for me in little over one year.

All I knew about Sacramento was that it was the capital of California and that it was located in the hot inland valley. I was quite terrified of having to make another adjustment to new surroundings. Furthermore, I thought there was no guarantee that our financial situation would be better in California than it was in New York. At least here we had relatives who could help us out if needed, and we were sure of a roof over our heads. Out West, we knew hardly anyone who might help us should Father not find work. It was clear, however, that my parents had already made up their minds, So I did not raise any real objections. I think my sister felt much the same way I did; but she acquiesced also.

Only a few days later we packed our belongings and left for the West. We went via the Trailways bus line, I think because its tickets were slightly cheaper than those of the competing Greyhound line. The bus left at five in the morning. It was pitch black and it seemed to me as if we were sneaking out in the middle of the night, like thieves in the dark.

1940-1943: Sacramento.

We had spent time pouring over an atlas in the library plotting the route our bus was going to take: Chicago, Kansas City, Denver, Salt Lake City, then over the Sierra Nevada to Sacramento. Some of these names I had read and fantasized about, others I had seen as Hollywood images. But neither books nor movies prepared me for the reality of the American landscape. As we crossed the country, I loved the enormity of the Rockies, the glowing granite amid the snow of the Sierra, the desolateness of the Great Salt Lake. But above all I could hardly believe the vastness of the country. In Holland and in Belgium space was at a premium. Farms were small, carefully defined by fences or rock barriers, villages separated from each other by short distances. Here on the immense Prairie were snow-covered farms that I knew grew wheat in the summer. In size at least, these appeared to me to be rural estates. As we traveled further west, cattle wandered seemingly without physical limitations in areas where there was no sign of human habitation. I thought that perhaps some of the ranches that we passed were the size of small European countries.

For long stretches the bus traveled on two lane roads over landscapes that hardly changed. Lucie and I amused ourselves by following the Burma Shave advertisements: different pithy, humorous sayings spread over several signs along the road, followed by the final sign with its invariant admonition. "Use Burma Shave". At other times I sat in my seat, either reading or daydreaming, worrying about our future, agonizing about having to go to a new school, fearing the impact of a new environment.

The bus stopped for meals at lunch counters or diners where the "Eats" signs blinked day and night. I recall our first breakfast. We sat on stools at a counter and I looked at an array of small white and colored boxes of cereals; Corn Flakes I knew, but here were also Wheaties, breakfast of champions, Rice Crispies, snap crackle and pop, Shredded Wheat, strength in every bite, and I had to chose. I don't remember which I had first, but by the time we reached our destination, I had tried them all. In Utah, in a small town where we stopped for lunch, the friendly and talkative counterman, hearing that we were new arrivals in the States, simply said: "Welcome to God's country," while not far away, in Nevada, a surly waitress mumbled something about "we don't need no more foreigners around here;

ain't enough work for us Americans". I began to worry about the way Sacramentans might feel about us.

Our last stop was in Truckee, just inside California. It was bitterly cold and snow was piled everywhere, hardly how I had pictured the Golden State. We were sitting in a restaurant, eating hamburgers for dinner. They were the cheapest items on the menu. The bus driver, a tall, sun burnt and athletic looking young man, sat with us. He had heard us talking about our destination and, I guess our accents and occasional lapses into German had made it obvious that we were new comers. He regaled us with stories of the beauty of the Sierra and particularly about a lake, Lake Tahoe.

"It's the most beautiful lake I know. And only twenty miles from here. Perhaps one day I can show it to you." He was looking directly at Lucie.

It dawned on me that my sister had become a very attractive, tall young woman: blue, wide-open eyes, blond hair, almost classic features, and a ready and winning smile. I think her English accent also added to her appeal. I remembered that in Vienna, in grade school, it was she who was chosen for a pageant celebrating Austrian heritage. She had to recite a poem that started like this: "I am a German girl, my eyes are blue and blond my hair."

In Sacramento a group of local Jews, with help from labor groups, had collected enough money to rent a small house for us. Not only did they pay for our rent, but also loaned us money until Father found work. Occasionally, strangers came to our house with food. "Welcome" they would say. And often: "If we can be of help, let us know." We were amazed at the friendliness and openness of our Western hosts. The contrast to the suspicious, xenophobic Europeans and the impersonal, often harsh New Yorkers was striking. The first few days after our arrival the sun shone brightly; this was followed by rains of an intensity we had never encountered. Flowers and flowering shrubs were everywhere. The market near our house was full of oranges and other fruits and vegetables that were rarities in Europe and, in winter, incredibly expensive in New York. It all seemed quite exotic to us. I thought that there was much more of a difference between Sacramento and what little I knew of the American East, than between the East and Europe.

The first day that I went to my new school, California Junior High it was appropriately called, I wore my best clothes: knee high socks, brightly polished shoes, a long sleeved shirt and knicker pants. This would not have been an unusual costume in Europe,

102

or even in New York, but in Sacramento all the students stared at me. They were all wearing sneakers, tee shirts and long pants. No one teased me about my attire or made fun of my limited English, but nevertheless I felt like a monkey on display. As soon as I could, I 'borrowed' two dollars from my parents and bought myself a pair of long pants. I looked at the sun burnt, healthy California kids, and was struck by the difference between their appearance and those of European or New York students. I wanted to emulate them. I vowed to myself that I would never cry in class again. Somehow I managed to keep my promise.

School I found incredibly boring. The European schools and the one in New York that I had attended were academically far more rigorous than those in Sacramento. I found that I was well ahead of my classmates in almost all subjects, except of course English, and I was quickly tagged as a nerd. I could not share my fellow students' enthusiasm for football or baseball, or other sports, and their social events appeared to me to be childish and even silly. Although most students were quite friendly, their concerns did not overlap with mine and our interests rarely intersected. To my male classmates' absolute shock, I could not identify all the cars on the road nor could I distinguish by sound a V-8 engine from an in-line 6. I did not know how to dance, nor did I want to learn; this did not endear me to the girls. Out of boredom I sometimes nodded off in class. My teachers were not too appreciative of what they considered my lack of respect.

Worst of all for me, nobody seemed to care about events in Europe; the few times I attempted discuss the war or the developing Holocaust with either teachers or students, I encountered either complete ignorance or what seemed to me to be incredibly callous indifference. These were usually good and nice people; they simply could not be bothered with events that were occurring outside their immediate surroundings. Once I told one of my teachers that Father had been arrested and had spent time in a concentration camp. "What was his crime?" the teacher wanted to know. Americans, lucky Americans, were used to the supremacy of the law. They simply could not believe that people could be rounded up, arrested and kept in prison and even killed for no reason other than their religion. This was consistent with the feeling of religious tolerance that seemed to be a staple of life in Northern California. Not once during my stay in Sacramento did I personally encounter an act of anti-Semitism.

My sister's experience in school was quite different. She fitted into her new environment with ease. Her social activities in school, dances, plays, a widening circle of friends, kept her occupied. As a result, although we were still on the best of terms, we hardly ever had any serious conversations. Father soon started to work as a gardener, taking minor jobs whenever and wherever he could find them. In Europe he had never been interested in plants; but now he read books about gardening and forced himself to learn about his new occupation. I did not appreciate how hard it must have been for him. In Vienna, he was Herr Hahn, respected owner of a business and supervisor of twenty or more employees. In Sacramento he was Jakob, and bossed no one. Except me. Not only did he attempt to reassert his absolute authority over me, but also he expected me to help him every day after school. Initially, I did not object. Gardening appealed to me and the thought of earning money, for me or for the family, was even more enticing. Unfortunately, Father frequently gave me incomplete or conflicting instructions. Then, if I did not do precisely what he had expected, his temper flared. Then he would threaten me and occasionally hit me. I came to dread these afternoons and their frequent aftermath's, and started to look for a job of my own. I became a delivery boy for the afternoon paper, the Sacramento Bee. No longer did I have to work for Father. Our battles at the dinner table continued, perhaps with less frequency, but if anything with more intensity. I started to invent excuses for not being home at mealtime. Mother watched our deteriorating relationship, but was helpless to influence its course. She was busy making a new life for herself, forcing herself to read books in English; our English-German dictionary seemed to find a permanent spot on her night table. For the first time in her life she became active in Jewish affairs and worked to raise money for refugee organizations.

One morning, in May of 1940, Father woke me up. He was very agitated.

"The Nazis have invaded Holland and Belgium." He showed me the headline in the Sacramento Union.

The invasion had made the front pages of both of the Sacramento papers. The radio networks also provided extensive coverage. Our family sat around the radio for many hours hoping to hear of successful defense by the invaded countries. But the news became worse and worse. When Holland and Belgium, later even France surrendered after only a few days' resistance, we were all devastated. Were the Germans invincible? Perhaps they truly were the master race.

I started to think about the fate of the children that had been my companions in Holland. I had received a few letters from the camp and even answered one or two. After the German occupation there was only silence. Not much later, horror stories started to appear in the Sacramento press, again on page 6, about mass murders of Jews in German occupied Poland. These were largely downplayed by the pundits, who likened the reports to exaggerated tales of German atrocities during World War I. Initially these dispatches didn't make a great impression on me. But, as the reports were repeated over and over again, I started dreaming about the children in the camp in Holland; more and more frequently I wondered about their existence. Faces started to appear in my dreams almost nightly: Eva, the girl who had been on the train with me going to The Hague; Hans, an older boy who had sworn that if the Germans came to Holland he would kill a few before he was killed himself; Heinz, a smallish boy who was a good ball player, liked to play chess and became my close friend, little Erna who had visited her parents on the island off the Belgian coast.

After the German invasion of Russia, the news about European Jews became steadily worse. Stories of mass exterminations and deportations became routine. One of the local papers devoted an editorial to the subject. It said essentially that while these reports were indeed horrifying, there was no proof that they were correct. Nazis may be bad, but the Germans were far too civilized to permit atrocities of this nature. Even if some excesses occurred, there was, in the Editor's view, no need for American involvement. It was the time of 'Lend Lease', when Roosevelt had prodded his administration and Congress to 'loan' ships and other weapons to the hard pressed British. The editorial suggested that America was already doing more than its share to rescue once again the arrogant and ungrateful Europeans. It was an opinion many Sacramentans heartily endorsed.

About this time my dreams started to become nightmares. The repeated basic theme was that I was attacked by Nazis who wanted to drag me and other children off to imprisonment. I fought as hard as I could to escape, but rarely successfully. I began to feel that Jews were inferior, bound to be exterminated by victorious Nazis. After such nightmares I frequently woke up on the floor of my room. My bed was in complete turmoil, with blankets, sheets and pillows tossed together into one common, messy pile. These nightmares stayed with me for many years, well into my married life, though their intensity decayed slowly. My wife quickly learned to get out of my way when, in the middle of the night I started to thrash about in what appeared to her as uncontrolled fury. In my freshman year in high school the nightmares became so vivid and frightening that I attempted to ward off sleep as long as possible. I read deep into the night until I was so tired that I hoped that nothing would disturb my sleep. I was not selective; almost any form of printed matter would do. Serious literature, pulp, pornography, magazines, newspaper classified advertisements.

My parents must have been extremely worried about their many relatives left in Europe. Father had not heard from his many sisters in months; Mother's mother now lived in Rumania with two her sons. Occasionally we still received letters from them. The letters did not come directly, but through an intermediary in Switzerland. The news was not good. They had very little food then and saw no hope for the future. While there were no Germans in the country, the local fascists lost no opportunity to make life miserable for the Romanian Jews.

I did not tune in to my parents' fears and worries. I was too preoccupied with my own.

In 1941, after Japan's attack on Pearl Harbor, the isolationist attitude changed quickly. The war became personal to almost everyone. By then, however, I had become so much the outsider that I rarely discussed what were my deepest concerns with anyone. This extended to my family.

I did enjoy my hours in the libraries. Sacramento had not only a reasonably good city public library, but also was the site of the California State Library, then a truly remarkable depository of thousands of books. After I had read almost everything in the former, one of the city librarians wrote me a note that enabled me to get a card for the State facility. Here I frequently went mornings when I was supposed to be in school. I came quite inventive in composing excuses that explained my absences, and it was not too difficult to forge Mother's name to these.

Pearl Harbor did not change my family's life appreciably, except that our finances improved. It became easier for Father to find work as a gardener, especially after all the Japanese were either interned or forced to leave the West Coast. Additionally, he thought it his duty to perform tasks he would normally have shunned. Many evenings he worked as a laborer for the Southern Pacific railroad, loading railroad cars with war materials. This after working a full day in other peoples' gardens. He did this for patriotic reasons and out of a desire to contribute to the defeat of the Nazis; but his labor also brought in extra money.

Mother found a job keeping books for a second hand store that was located at the interface between what I later found out were the two Sacramentos. It was owned by an unsavory character who paid her a very low wage and abused her verbally for keeping the books too carefully. Apparently he had hired her thinking that as a European Jew she would be good at doctoring his records in order to hide his profits from the tax collector.

The news from Europe was getting worse and worse. The Germans had advanced deep into Russia and appeared unstoppable. It was not clear if or how long the British could hold out under the daily bombardment by the German airforce. I began to fear more and more that the picture painted by German propaganda of the Aryan Superman was indeed true. And, even worse, that their continually trumpeted inferiority of Jews was also correct. In the mornings, when I looked in the mirror, was I looking at the kind of creature portrayed in the Nazi hate-literature?

The Jewish tragedy in Europe continued its gruesome and sepulchral progression. The Jewish newspaper was overflowing with horror tales. Reports of mass killings of men, women and children by special German units in the East became commonplace. Rumors of the construction of large concentration camps in Poland started to appear. And Jews from all over Europe, from Holland, Belgium, France, everywhere, were being rounded up. These tales terrified me, but I read them with a morbid and addictive fascination. Very often after reading of the Nazi's demonic activities, I would have particularly bad nightmares.

When I came home from school now, the house was empty. Father and Mother were at work, and my sister was involved in various school-related social activities. One day, however, when I rode my bicycle home, I found Mother's bedroom door closed. Listening at the door, I could hear her crying and sobbing. I didn't know what to do. Never had I heard her like this.

She talked to herself in German, about her mother, her brother. At times she yelled: "They all want to kill us"; or "Why am I here? I wish I were dead!" Then she sobbed again. I knocked on the door. "Leave me alone" was the only response and that only after I had knocked repeatedly and tried to talk to her several times. Then our back door opened, and Father came in. He started talking to Mother through the closed door. His voice was quiet and coaxing as he urged her, in German, to open the door to let him in, to help her. He could be amazingly gentle with her.

"What happened? Is it my grandmother? Has anything happened to her?" I didn't know what to expect.

"There was a letter. Mutti called me. It's from Rumania. I saw it on the kitchen table. Read for yourself and then you won't have to ask so many questions."

He didn't have to be gentle with me. Mother's door opened. I only got a glimpse of her tear covered, very pale face, her disheveled hair, and her clothes in disarray. She was holding a large blue handkerchief to her nose. She did not look at me.

"Ach, Jakob," she was shaking as she reached out to him, "They all want to kill us" she repeated. Father put his arms around her, and talked to her quietly. She continued crying and sobbing and only gradually quieted down.

The letter, open on the kitchen table, was from Rumania, although the envelope was franked with Swiss stamps. I had difficulty making out the handwriting; the letters were small and squeezed together. It was written in rather poor German and many of the words were illegible because parts the thin airmail paper had somehow become wet and the ink had run badly. But its message was unmistakable and the first words set the tone:

"Such news no one should have to write…"

The writer first described the death of my grandmother. She had fled Vienna and was living with Mother's oldest brother and his family in a provincial Romanian town that was later annexed by the Soviet Union but now is part of the Ukraine. Living conditions became worse as the war progressed, and food was rationed at near starvation levels. Jews received even less than the general population. My grandmother insisted, according to the letter, that at least half her meager provisions be divided among my two teen-aged cousins. As a result she became progressively emaciated and finally died of chronic malnutrition. Starvation is a less polite term.

After her death my aunt and uncle decided that they had to leave Romania at all costs. No avenues of escape, however, seemed available. Desperately, they and perhaps two hundred other Jews rented an old freighter, the Struma, to take them to Palestine. I assume Rumanian authorities had to be bribed to allow the ship to take on its passengers, men, women and children, and leave for the port of Haifa. The British, who were then administrating Palestine under mandate of the fore-runner of the United Nations, the weak and ineffectual League of Nations, had solemnly promised to facilitate making that country a homeland for the Jewish people.

Every nook and cranny of the old tub was filled with people. Among them were my aunt, uncle and my two teenage cousins. Although I doubt that the trip resembled a Mediterranean pleasure cruise, the ship did make it at least as far as Turkey. The British governor of Palestine, in spite of his country's promise to facilitate immigration, refused permission for any of the passengers to disembark. To war time Britain, Arab oil was certainly more important than Jewish lives. After several days of futile negotiations, the ship was ordered to return to Rumania. On its way back it was said to hit one of the many mines floating in this war torn area, although recent reports suggest that it may have been sunk by a Russian submarine. Except for one man, there were no survivors. Mother's brother, his wife, my two young cousins all drowned. In an Orwellian inversion of reality, the Rumanian government, whose minions were actively starving and killing Jews, used this event to demonstrate the evilness of the British and paraded it as a partial justification for having effected Rumania's earlier entry into the war on Germany's side.

I could only partially share Mother's extreme grief. My grandmother was old and although I certainly loved her, there were so many young people dying. My uncle and his family I only knew from their infrequent visits to Vienna. They were relatives, but also strangers. Their tragedy did strongly reinforce my developing contempt for all authority: Father, school, the police, the British or Rumanians, the Nazis.

In 1943 I obtained a new job after school and evenings delivering and accepting telegrams for a company called Postal Telegraph, an unsuccessful competitor of Western Union. This job provided me with an education about the city that had become our new home.

In the small towns of the West then no one lived in apartments. And Sacramento was a small town. With few exceptions, its streets were not named, but were tagged by numbers or letters. It had a population of over fifty thousand, which made it the third or fourth largest community in California, but in spirit and soul it was more of a village than a city. Or, rather, two villages.

The state employees, augmented by the usual coterie of merchants and artisans, formed a tight community, somewhat suspicious of strangers and not necessarily welcoming to newcomers. Most of our early visitors had been either newcomers themselves, or outsiders who for personal or religious reasons were not accepted by the local society. They occupied the 'good' eastern and southern parts of town that were characterized by expansive green lawns, punctuated by old and often beautiful trees, surrounding houses that ranged from modest to quite luxurious. The older houses had wooden facades, usually freshly painted; the newer and more costly ones were covered by bright, white stucco. New or old, the houses were separated from those on either side by gardens and fences. Flowers and flowering trees were everywhere. In these sections of town, a bastion of the middle class, people lived comfortable, self-satisfied lives and were essentially isolated from the problems of their neighbors and of the rest of the world. A political science professor from the local junior college who became my parents' good friend, was well acquainted with the local scene told us:

"Crime are banished to the 'bad' parts of town," he told us. "The police insure this by quickly arresting any 'vagrants' who find their way into our part of town." Indeed, we found that crime in our area was almost non-existing. It came almost as a shock to us when we discovered that we never needed to lock our doors, or that milk or other items delivered early in the morning remained undisturbed at our front door even if we were gone for most or all of the day.

The other part of Sacramento presented a jarring contrast. Gamblers, prostitutes, alcoholics, seasonal farm hands looking for any available work, and other drifters constituted its population. These lived primarily in the West End, in an area of perhaps twenty to thirty city blocks. The first time that I went there, several weeks after our arrival, I immediately saw and felt familiar terrain. This was the Wild West I had seen in Vienna at countless Saturday afternoon movie matinees. Here were run down, wooden two-story houses either unpainted or with faded paint that peeled off in small and, in some places large flakes. Wide porches ran the lengths of the second stories and partially shaded the sidewalks from the powerful rays of the hot valley sun. No gardens or other spaces separated these dwellings. Interspersed among the many saloons, bookie joints and whorehouses were small stores, some with Spanish signs, and others with Oriental symbols. The many bars had swinging doors and, particularly in the evenings, stumbling drunks were pushed out by heavy barkeeps. It could have been a movie set. Only the horses were missing and guns were not carried, at least openly.

In this part of the city crime flourished. Gangsters managed gambling and prostitution; and they controlled their terrain ruthlessly. The newspapers, I was told, seldom reported mob killings. The police did not interfere in these internecine struggles as long as violence did not occur openly or spill over into the respectable part of the city. During the day there was very little interchange between the two Sacramentos. After dark, however, a stream of respectable citizens found pleasures in the seedy gambling joints and brothels of the West End.

This situation was tailor made for a petty form of blackmail. Late at night, we delivery boys would take turns going to the houses of ill repute.

"Somebody called for Postal Telegraph service," we claimed loudly but falsely. Invariably, either the madam or one of the johns gave us a dollar and told us to get lost, which we happily did. No one wanted a commotion that would compel the complaisant and corrupt cops to take action that might lead to the embarrassment of prominent citizens. I suspect that the madams were well aware of our scam, but in the Wild West there was an attitude of live and let live, at least with respect to petty crime.

From a school friend, another outsider, I bought a hunting rifle, an old high-powered twenty-two. He owned a thirty four Plymouth coupe and he and I, and sometimes a third rebel, would go into the hills east of Sacramento and attempt to shoot rabbits and deer. At first I was a terrible shot, but as time went by, I got to the point where I would occasionally hit my target. We began to extend our trips to the Sierra Nevada, a hundred miles to the east. One evening, after an unsuccessful day's hunt, we camped on the shore of Lake Tahoe; 'the most beautiful lake in the world', as the bus driver had described it. Our campfire was the only light visible on the entire lake. During the war the few scattered cabins that then existed were tightly shuttered and tourism was non-existent.

Sometimes we were gone for several days. With the onset of war, gasoline had become severely rationed. We replenished our dwindling supplies by siphoning it from State road maintenance vehicles. These, after work hours and on weekends, were parked by the side of the road and we could steal gas without much fear of detection. Hunting quickly started to interfere with school. My grades were slipping badly and my forged excuses for my absences from school were no longer accepted.

1943: Rebellion.

The visit of the truant officer had become a frequent event that Mother dreaded. The first few times he came, it was always the same man, she tried to make excuses for me, lied, claimed that I was ill. I never met the officer, but I can reconstruct, from her descriptions, how mother saw his visits.

"I am sure that you don't like to see my face again." The man seemed nice enough, he smiled and his voice did not have that Western harshness that made English into a language difficult to understand, at least in Mother's view. He did have hard, blue eyes and these suggested a discrepancy between his interior and his exterior.

"George has not been to school the last three days. I tried to telephone here earlier in the day but there was no answer. Are you still working? George isn't at school again, hasn't been for three days. And he is obviously not at home. So I've got to assume that he is truant again."

Lately she had not been willing to lie, shoulder the responsibility for making excuses for me. She had not told Father of my first few disappearances from school, not wanting to worsen the already tense relationship that had developed between him and me. After an earlier confrontation, during which I had questioned his authority, he had threatened to send me to a correctional institution. When on that occasion he also severely beat me, I told him that if he ever did that again, I would simply leave home. After my year in Holland I knew, or at least believed, that I could take care of myself. These fights horrified Mother. She frequently took my side during the clashes and I thus became the cause of their otherwise rare arguments.

"Oh, yes, I must work. But George is not a juvenile delinquent; he has his problems but..."

But what? She was beginning to wonder.

The man was not too sympathetic. He disliked dealing with foreigners. They were either not aware of the law or didn't care about their kids' education. Many regarded the authorities, school or otherwise, as their enemies. Worst were the Mexicans. They didn't even want to learn English. Luckily, there were not too many of their kind in Sacramento. And almost all of them lived in the western part of town. With the bookies, Chinamen, and whores.

Why their kids were allowed to go to school in the first place, he could not understand. Field hands, that's all they were good for. Why the bureaucrats that ran the local schools cared was another mystery. If folks didn't want an education, like the Oakies, screw-em. Let em stay home. He didn't really like being a truant officer, but a job was a job.

These people here were something else. Australian. Or was it Austrian? As if it really mattered. He had been here several times before. The kid skipped school. He had never met the father. The woman was difficult to find at home during regular hours. She had a job somewhere, but where or what she did he did not know. Nor did he really care. Women should stay home and take care of their children. He wouldn't allow his wife to work, that was for sure.

The woman spoke English with a thick German accent. When she was excited her vocabulary shrank, and then she substituted German words and idioms when her memory did not produce the appropriate English expression.

"He took his... Gewehr... How do you say... his rifle... and went shooting. For deer. I don't know how he can like killing animals. He left a note. Here is it. He and his father had a big fight. A man should not hit such a big boy. Now I do not know where George is. Somewhere in the mountains."

The few words that were written didn't say much other than that the kid had gone to the mountains. The truant officer thought of going hunting in the Sierra. Not alone, with his old man. He well recalled the thrill of shooting his first buck. And the praise from his father. But this woman seemed to think that hunting was some sort of a crime. Foreigners have strange notions. But in any case this was not his concern. The kid had to obey regulations.

"He and you know that he has to go to school", he said more or less for the record. The truant officer, as his job required, had acquainted himself with my school history. Until about a year ago, no problems. Now, five truancies in the last six months. Something had happened, he was pretty sure. Perhaps the father did not take the kid out to the woods enough, perhaps he should be a Boy Scout leader, teach the kid fishing.

"All children have occasional fights with their fathers; especially boys. And an occasional whack never hurt nobody. Anyway, that's no excuse for just taking off! What's the matter with the kid?"

Tears were in her eyes. "I really don't know what to do. He has so changed so much in the last years."

"Look lady, here is my card." The truant officer had to visit four more homes that afternoon. He could not waste any more time. "If he ain't home within the next three days, that is by Sunday, gimme a call. I am in the office between nine and ten thirty. Monday through Friday. I'd like to help, but if he ain't back by Monday we'll have to treat him as a runaway. If he does get back, make sure he goes to school Monday. Either you or your husband go with him. I'll get hold of him there. "

"I am sure he'll be here by then. Never has he more than three days stayed away. "

"There is always a first time." The man didn't mean to sound mean or pessimistic, but in his experience, once kids started to stay away from home several days at a time, then things rapidly went from bad to worse. The distance from truant to delinquent was usually very short. Mother was now crying openly. The man regretted his last remark. He did not like to see women cry.

"Look, lady, I've seen kids do much worse things. Even some of those still straighten out. Don't get all upset now. Your son is a smart kid and one of these days he'll turn around." He didn't actually believe what he said, but perhaps this would stop the tears.

"I hope I won't have hear from you Monday. Still if he ain't home by then, don't forget to call me. Your husband and you are responsible for him. Now, please, sign this here form. All it says is that I have talked to you and that you understand what you have to do. You've seen this paper before. It ain't changed since last time." She signed without bothering to read the print.

"Good by." He turned, walked to his car, a gray Ford coupe with Sacramento school district markings stenciled in black on the doors.

"I bet that kid will be in jail before too long", he thought to himself as he drove off.

1943: The Mafia.

It was not only hunting that kept me from going to school. I started to spend more and more time in the West end of town. Pinball machines that required a nickel per game were found in the pool halls, smoke shops and bookie joints, fascinated me. These were an early form of electronic toy. Playing them also involved a rather primitive element of gambling. With some skill and much luck it was possible to win free replays. These could be converted to nickels by motioning surreptitiously to the man behind the counter or the bar; who would then come to the machine, record the number of games, and reach under the device to press a secret button that returned the free game register to zero. For each free game, a nickel. In California, gambling devices were strictly against the law. But then so were book making, selling of cigarettes and liquor to minors, and various other forms of vice that went on quite openly under the benevolent eyes of the guardians of Sacramento law.

The odds against actually winning money on any of the machines were enormous. I soon found this out as all my earnings disappeared into the nickel slots. In order to get more money to keep the metal balls spinning, I started looking for coins in our house, even emptying Mother's purse and taking change from my sister. All the money that I could lay my hands on went to turn on the flashing lights, hear strange electronic noises and watch the metal balls connect, or more frequently not connect, with score-producing barriers and knobs and other targets. The machines mesmerized me. I played, or watched others play, for hours at a time. Lights and sounds blotted out thoughts and anxieties even more effectively than did my compulsive reading.

In my junior year in high school things went from bad to worse. A truant officer started to come to our house more and more frequently. My grades plummeted even further and my relationship with Father deteriorated to the point where we hardly spoke. I attempted to be out of the house whenever I thought that he would be there. Once the police accused me of stealing a bicycle; I hadn't actually done so, but knew who had. As a first offender, I was let go with only a warning.

Towards the end of that school year, I became tired of losing all my money to the pinball games. There must be ways of beating these devices, I thought. So I started to examine the various games for ways of cheating them. I devised several schemes: cutting springs to disable one of the machine's protective devices; loosening the screws that held the glass plate that covered the slanting table on which the balls selected their paths, so that I could insert a small metal rod and continually agitate a score-producing knob. Now money started flowing my way. But my schemes were countered. Somebody reworked the machines so that I could no longer loosen the glass. Springs were protected or placed in positions that cutting or manipulating them no longer gave me an advantage.

It became a game of cat and mouse. I wrote to the manufacturers of the pinball games claiming that I was an electrician and needed wiring diagrams for repair purposes. To my amazement, two manufacturers sent me these without asking any questions. From the diagrams I learned that I could drill holes in the sides of the machines and then insert my metal rods to agitate mechanical relays.

One rainy Friday evening, after what had now become a routinely successful raid on the pinball empire, I was riding my bicycle home. Two men in a forty-one Chevy, by now even I could recognize all cars and models, forced me to the curb. One of them grabbed my bike, while the other got out of the car. He was carrying a baseball bat. I was very terrified. 'Mob enforcers', I immediately thought.

"You better listen good," the man carrying the bat said to me. "We don't wanna have to beat up no kid".

"Yeah", the other one added "but you've been screwing around with them pinballs. Trying to screw us, you little shit. You stay away from them things. They ain't for kids nohow. It ain't legal." The irony of his appeal to the law did not penetrate any of us. The man with the bat took a swing at the back wheel of my bike. I could hear an almost musical sound as several of the tightly strung spokes snapped.

"That won't feel so hot on your legs. Them bones break easy." The man released my bike, and the two got back into their car. The driver, the man who had swung the bat, stuck his head out the window:

"Next time we ain't gonna go so easy on you," he yelled as they drove off.

I was shaking with fear. My West Sacramento acquaintances had told me too many stories about the mob's methods of enforcing its rule. I tried to get on my bike. Although it did not seem to be damaged too badly, I could not ride it. The back wheel had become egg shaped. I locked the frame against a lamppost. It was too late in the evening for busses to be running, so I was forced to walk home in the rain. I did not stop shaking until I was in my bed with my blankets pulled over me.

The next day I repaired my bike; a used wheel cost me a dollar and a half. The following week I attended school religiously. I was too frightened to go to work or, after school, to leave our house. Evenings I stayed in my room, reading and doing homework. I had told no one of my encounter, certainly not the police.

The next Friday, shortly after I had come home from school, our front door bell rang. I looked out the window and to my dismay I recognized the goon who had wielded the bat. Now he was without weapons, and I must admit, his face really didn't look particularly mean. He could have been a waiter, or a high school teacher, for that matter.

"I did just what you told me; I stayed away from the pinballs," I said as my teeth began to chatter.

"Yeah, I know. Lookee, ain't no need for you to be scared. I ain't come to do you no harm. The boss, he seems to think you are a pretty smart cookie. He thinks maybe we could do some business. But first, he figures I ought to pay you for your bike. How much they soak you to get it fixed?"

I told him.

"Maybe you ain't as smart as the boss thinks. Maybe you are a pretty dumb kid after all. If youda told me five, I'da given you a fin."

He spoke as if he'd been listening to too many gangster movies. He handed me two dollars.

"Keep the four bits. But if you wanna be smart, always take care of number one. Ain't nobody else gonna do it". Apparently he did not consider that I might be too scared to even think about taking care of number one.

The money went into my pocket. What did he really want from me? I didn't have to wait long.

"Oh yeah!" He remembered why he had come. "What the boss says is for you to come down to our place where the new machines come in. He figures that you can look at 'em and maybe find ways to crack 'em and then tell us how to fix things so that smart asses like you can't steal our dough. Ten bucks a pop he'll give you. Not bad, eh?"

He smiled, showing a set of perfectly white teeth. I always thought all gangsters would have yellow, tobacco stained dentures. Somehow his white teeth made him less of a threat.

"You be here mañana at this time. I'll pick you up. Don't keep the boss waiting. He don't like it." He turned around and walked away. Obviously, it never occurred to him that I might refuse. Nor did it to me. I was too scared. So I started to work for the mob. I looked at pinball games from the outside and the inside. I figured our how relays could be activated, how holes could be drilled in the side of machines to insert metal rods, and how springs and plungers might be manipulated to increase the players' odds. Most were unlikely scenarios, but true to the man's word, each one was worth ten dollars. After seven or eight such 'pops', I was told that my services were no longer needed. No reason was given and I didn't ask for any. Although I missed the money, I was greatly relieved to be able to sever my connections with the mob without ill aftereffects.

Perhaps I was dismissed because the West End of town was changing. As the war progressed and slowly turned to the Allies' favor, the Air Force established several bases near Sacramento. The military threatened to make the city 'Off Limits' to uniformed personnel if the brothels were not closed, open gambling ended, and the sale of liquor to minors did not cease. All the local young men were in uniform and many overseas, so migrant workers now readily found jobs. Hence the transient population dwindled. The bars were still full, but the customers were now primarily uniformed and bartenders rarely tried to evict them from the saloons. The police began to enforce laws more strictly, perhaps even those related to pinball machines. Perhaps the city fathers had decided that the money spent by the servicemen in local businesses outweighed the revenue generated by prostitution and gambling.

In an ironic way my interaction with the Mafia changed my life. No longer did I play pinball machines; I still feared the mob. With part of the money I had earned, I bought a car for fifteen dollars, a Model A Ford. It had been in an accident and the driver's side was damaged so badly that its door could not be opened. I had to get in via the passenger side and then scoot over to get behind the steering wheel. The car had one great advantage, Its spark was adjustable, so that when turned to its optimum position, the Ford to ran on 'white gas', a solvent intended for cleaning purposes that was not rationed. Stealing became unnecessary.

My newly found interest in electrical devices caused me to apply for a job as an electrician apprentice at the Sacramento repair yards of the Southern Pacific Railroad. Here railroad engines were overhauled and refitted. In peacetime the highly valued apprentice positions were tightly controlled by the electricians' union and were awarded only after several years' work as a lowly electrician's helper. During the war, however, there was such a shortage of workers that I was taken on immediately. I was told, however that I might lose my job, once returning veterans demanded reinstatement. My days were now full: school until early in the afternoon and then an eight, sometimes even a ten-hour shift in the yard.

I had not lost my Socialist naivete. While I did not expect to find a worker's paradise, I was certainly not prepared for what I did encounter at the railroad shops. Work rules were rigid and tightly enforced by stewards from several AFof L craft unions: electricians, mechanics, boilermakers. Each union guarded its turf jealously, a practice that led to absurd situations. For example, electricians were not allowed to touch wrenches. Only mechanics were allowed to work with these tools. Not infrequently the journey man electrician, my mentor, and I encountered electrical connections enclosed in boxes whose covers were held in place by nuts and bolts. If we could not open these with a pair of pliers, union rules required us to call for a mechanic. Often we had to wait an hour or more before we could start our work.

The railroad shops had only been unionized for four or five years, and that after a bitter strike. All the old timers told horror stories of earlier management arrogance and abuse of power. These workers considered the union rules their only protection against the bosses, and hence regarded them as highly or perhaps higher than they did the Ten Commandments. Even in wartime.

My boss, a man in his forties, had a son who was fighting in the Pacific.

"Don't you think that these rules ought to be relaxed? Don't you feel that they impede the war effort against Japan?" The Southern Pacific railroad carried a large fraction of the war materials and personnel destined for the Asian war.

The electrician looked at me as though I had blasphemed. "You don't know what the hell you are talking about."

At seven in the evening the swing shift, my shift, had its supper break. I sometimes ate the sandwiches that I had brought from home with another electrician, a small dark haired fellow in his fifties. When I first met him I thought he was a hunchback. When he walked he would grimace, as though each step was an ordeal. A physician had told him that he had curvature of the spine and that it was bound to get worse as he grew older. This man was the only avowed Communist that I ever encountered in Sacramento. His reading matter seemed to consist entirely of the People's World, the San Francisco party organ. I had become disillusioned with Soviet style communism ever since the German-Russian treaty of 1939 and the subsequent division of Poland. I listened to the twists and turns of this man's mind with curiosity and an almost scientific detachment.

"What do you think of all the union rules that slow down the work that we do?" I asked him.

"The AFL unions are all run by revisionist, corrupt fascists, as bad as the Mafia." Anybody he did not like was a fascist. Revisionists, I gathered, was a term used by the Communists for those on the left not smitten by Stalin and the Worker's paradise.

"They are almost as bad as the fascist bosses". He then told me about specific business agents of union locals that he had encountered who had 'betrayed the interests of the workers'. Not only corruption, but also any compromise that did not follow the Party Line was a betrayal.

"Were you at the yard during The Strike?" When you worked at the railroad yard there was only one strike.

"What do you think? I have worked here for seventeen years! And I was a union member and organizer most of that time." He then waxed almost lyrically about the heroic workers and how they had defeated the imperialist capitalists who owned the railroad. "That's why we need the union rules, to protect us from them."

But on another day, perhaps after reading a new editorial in his Koran, he would declaim loudly that the fascist unions were impeding the war effort whose sole justification, according to him, was to save the workers' homeland, the sacred Soviet Union. He was a bitter man, not only because of his illness, but also because in spite of his long service, he had been shunted away from having any influence in union activities.

My job I found quite boring. I learned very little. Splicing wires, changing fuses, only a member of the electrician's union was allowed to change fuses, waiting for a mechanic to unscrew covers, that's how I seemed to spend my afternoons and evenings. A boring job was not what I needed. It left too much time for thinking, worrying.

Faces of the children I had left behind in Holland kept dancing in front of my eyes.

One of the work activities reserved for electricians and their apprentices was that of operating overhead cranes. Within my first week on the job I was shown how to operate these. When I asked why only electricians, I was told: "The cranes got electrical motors, ain't they?" Unassailable logic. As an apprentice, I substituted for operators, ill, or not appearing at work for other reasons. Absenteeism was high in the yard, in spite of the war. Running the cranes was a task I enjoyed. These machines looked like movable bridges, some twenty feet long. Most of them lumbered about fifteen feet above the shop area. The bridges moved on rails, one rail on each side of the narrow shops. Along each bridge, also on rails, one or two trolleys moved back and forth as controlled by the operator. Suspended from the trolleys with heavy cables were large hooks that could be lowered or raised by the operator who sat, or more often stood, in a gondola like structure suspended below one end of the bridge. It contained levers that independently controlled the motion of the bridge, the trolleys and the hook. When the bridge moved, the noise it made was not unlike that of a streetcar. Some of these cranes were so powerful that they could lift an entire railroad engine. The first time I was allowed to operate one of these monsters, I felt a real sense of power and responsibility. Others were much smaller and used primarily to move engine parts from one part of the shop to another. The motion of the crane was directed by a foreman or other lead man on the ground who used hand signals: move the bridge, roll the trolley along the bridge, up or down the hook. Watching for the hand signals required the crane operator's constant attention; a misreading could result in a serious accident.

The job was perfect for me. No time to think, to fear, to daydream about horrors in Europe. So when a permanent crane operators' job opened, I applied for it. Jobs in the yard were awarded strictly on the basis of seniority, another union rule, so I did not think I had much chance, but nobody else "bid" on this job; so it was awarded to me.

The crane that was my permanent home for about eight months was situated in the foundry. There, wheels for engines and also railroad cars were made on a continuous basis. Molten steel was poured into circular forms, and then the red-hot wheels were cooled in progressively shallower and hence cooler pits. The crane's bridge spanned the narrow arm of the rectangular foundry. It rolled about four or five feet above the hot sand that surrounded the pits. Instead of a hook at the end of its cables it had a needle-nose device that expanded when the cables were pulled taut. The job of the ground crew and myself was to keep the wheels moving from their place of initial formation to a destination in the foundry, where they were stacked for cleaning and sanding by the day shift.

My job was simple. I positioned the crane near one of the deep pits There one member of the ground crew, two older men in their late forties, grabbed the device at the end of the cable. I gave it enough slack so that he could drop it into one of the pits. The weighted needle nose front end entered into the axle holes of a stack of wheels. When I then rolled the cable back up on its drum, four of the red-hot wheels emerged from the pit.

The next step was to move the crane and drop the wheels into a more shallow, empty pit. There the other member of the ground crew freed the needle nose device, and I returned the crane to a deeper pit for a new load. Of course there were tricks to this operation. The most important was to force the wheels into a swinging motion so that I could drop them into the pit with exact timing., If I did it correctly, the men on the ground were exposed only for a short time to the intense heat of the wheels and the noxious fumes they gave off. During my first few days I frequently blundered. Sometimes I raised the wheels instead of lowering them, swung the wheels too far, or moved the crane into a wrong position. Each of these mishaps was greeted with loud curses in a language that I finally identified as Italian. But after a few days I became quite adept at my task and the curses ended.

The heat from the pits and the sulfurous smell given off by the molten steel did not make for a pleasant work environment. To compensate for our discomfort, we were allowed twenty minutes every two hours to recuperate. I spent most of that time talking to the two Italians. They both had come to the States from Sicily in the twenties, yet their English was still quite limited. After a few weeks they started treating me almost as a younger member of their family. Lots of advice, lots of good-natured kidding, primarily about sexual matters. And lots of stories. About the old country, about the old days in Sacramento, about the Southern Pacific Company, for which they had both worked for almost twenty years. I asked them about The Strike. They had remained on the job; I remembered that when I told my Communist friend that I was going to work in the foundry, his only comment had been: "So, you gonna work with them goddamned scabs. Watch your back, they carry knives."

While they had no love for the company, they thought they owed it loyalty for having provided them with work even during the years of the great depression. Furthermore they disliked the union bosses even more than the railroad management.

"They are only out for theirselves, to fill pockets with our money. We no want to give them nothing. Nothing but a bunch of crooks. Tell you somthin today, opposite tomorrow."

"Just like the Mafia at home," I said.

"No, no you crazy. Mafia capos have honor. When they make a promise, that's it. They keep word."

If they don't have you killed first, I thought to myself.

I benefited from my new job in a variety of ways. The amount of money I earned, more than a dollar an hour, seemed phenomenal. My pay at Postal Union had been 35 cents an hour. I did well on the job, the Italians told me so. That and the fact that they obviously liked me, suggested that in spite of German propaganda, I was not an inferior creature. I didn't have many fights with my father any more; I simply was not home enough. And I was too busy with work and school to worry obsessively about the fate of European Jews. Ironically, the interest in electrical things induced by my Mafia connection remained with me for much of the rest of my life, prompting me to take up physics when, after World War II, I entered the University of California.

1944-45: My War.

I graduated from high school in mid year, early in 1944. The war was going full blast. While the Allies had won important victories on land in Stalingrad, and in North Africa and at sea in the Pacific, it was clear that the bulk of the fighting lay ahead. I was anxious to become part of it. In any capacity. Not that I wanted to don a uniform or that I was anxious to be the target of bullets. Dealing with another layer of heavy-handed authority was also nothing I looked forward to. But more and more it became obvious that as a Jew this was my fight, and I thought I had to participate. I had heard that the Canadians allowed seventeen year olds to enlist in the Royal Canadian Airforce. Even before graduation from high school, I took off a day from work and hitchhiked to San Francisco to visit the Canadian consulate to find out how this could be done.

When I found the building, I told the receptionist what I wanted and she directed me to an office that had a wide open door. A young woman in uniform, blue if I remember correctly, welcomed me. She was very cordial.

"I understand you want to volunteer for the Canadian Forces. Unfortunately we have an agreement with the US government that prevents us from accepting US citizens."

"But I am not a U.S. citizen".

"Oh, well then we can go ahead." She smiled at me. "Are you over 18?"

"No, but almost".

"Almost doesn't count. You will have to get your parents' signature permitting you to enlist. Will they give you permission?"

Of course I said: "Yes," although I knew that my parents would insist I wait for my eighteenth birthday. I had forged my mother's signature often enough, and the thought of also forging my father's didn't particularly worry me.

"In that case we might as well start the paperwork."

She handed me several forms and I started to fill in the blanks. For non-British or non-Dominion citizens the first form I tackled asked for 'current passport'. I didn't know what to put down. My current passport was German, but I certainly didn't consider myself German. The document had a big red "J", for Jude, (Jew) stamped on its front page, which in my opinion made it more of a Jewish passport, though I knew very well that that had no legal standing. I thought that perhaps I should say "Austrian". Perplexed, I turned to the friendly Canadian for help. For reasons I still don't understand, her friendliness evaporated.

She looked up some regulation and then turned to me. "Austria no longer exists." She looked at me severely. "You are German and therefore an enemy alien. We don't allow enemy aliens to enlist in the Canadian army." So as far as Canada was concerned, I was an enemy.

When some months later I tried to enlist in the US army, the result was different but equally confusing. The American government did not recognize the validity of the Anschluss. It considered Austria a neutral country. My German passport was therefore issued illegally. To the American government I was an Austrian, and hence a citizen of a neutral country. Neutral aliens could not enlist in the US army.

"They can be drafted, but only voluntarily", the recruiting sergeant told me. No enemy of oxymorons, he.

Enemy or neutral, a few weeks later, shortly after my 18th birthday, I was 'voluntarily drafted'. That simply meant that I didn't take advantage of my status as a neutral alien to refuse entry into the US army.

I was officially inducted into the army at the Presidio of Monterey, in central California. From there I was sent to infantry basic training, not far away, at Camp Roberts, California.

In basic training I encountered something new: American anti-Semitism. Not that it affected me directly. I had learned my lesson well. Cheating and lying is the way to get along in the adult world. So when I was asked if I was Jewish, I vehemently denied it. I didn't look particularly Jewish, so I simply claimed that I had no religion at all. My fellow soldiers readily accepted my denials but personnel officers were offended by my refusal to associate myself with a recognized church. These seemed to think it their mission in life to make sure that all of the lowly enlisted men had a religion spelled out on their identification tags.

"Aren't you worried how you will be buried if you get killed?" one asked.

Another warned me that my parents would surely want to have me buried under a cross.

"After death God will judge you if you have denied him," a third warned me. But I stood my grounds and my dogtags showed that I had no religious preference.

My fellow trainees were a curious group. Most of them, perhaps seventy percent, came from the hills of Kentucky and Tennessee. They had just finished a twelve-week session at a camp called McQuaide where they were supposed to have absorbed the rudiments of reading and writing. Perhaps some did, but the majority could easily have qualified as certified illiterates. They were quite clannish, and suspicious of anyone not coming from their background. In the evenings they drank huge amounts of rotgut whiskey available in the neighboring town of Paso Robles. Sufficiently lubricated, they would unleash their guitars and sing hillbilly songs. Very often these were full of self-pity. The one I remember most was called 'The Post Man Brought a Letter' about a soldier killed in action. I hated the sentimentality of the song, detested its tune, and soon with it all hillbilly music.

Mexicans from the barrios in and around Los Angeles formed the second largest group. These were also clannish, though in a different way. Many did not know more than a smattering of English; they had no choice but to stick with others who spoke Spanish. I had taken Spanish in school and could communicate with the Mexicans in a very rudimentary way. At times I would be drafted to act as an interpreter. This led to pretty comical situations when I completely misunderstood the rapidly spoken Spanish, or uttered incomprehensible absurdities in that language.

There were also a few West Coast Anglos in the training company, perhaps six or seven. Two Jews, pale, small, dark hair and black eyes, from New York rounded off this odd combination. They were supposed to have gone to a technical program at the nearby Polytechnic school, but because of an Army snafu they ended up at Roberts in basic training. The anti-Semitism directed against them consisted primarily of verbal assaults. They were called Jewboys and Kikes to their faces and made social outcasts by all but three or four of the English-speaking soldiers. They were, however, never physically harmed.

I found American anti-Semitism different from its German cousin. It was mixed with a curious sense of fair play. For instance, as part of training, the Army instituted so called tolerance sessions. These, in my company, were led by the sergeant in charge of our training, a Texan who had seen considerable combat in the Pacific. He started out the first session:

"I hate niggers; I hate Jews. But you gotta admit they get a raw deal. They didn't ask to be born niggers or Jews."

The sergeant asked for a show of hands "Who hates Jews and niggers?" Almost all the soldiers from Kentucky and Tennessee raised their hands.

"Why do you hate Jews?" I guess his instruction manual told him to start a discussion. A few said that Jews were 'bloodsuckers' or 'too goddamn rich'; but the vast majority said: "they killed Christ". Two of the other Californians and I tried to argue. We quickly became known as Jewlovers and niggerlovers, though oddly enough this was not held against us.

One of the perks of being in uniform was that becoming an American citizen was made easy. I don't know the laws today, but in 1944 it required five years' of residence in the US before an immigrant could apply for citizenship. Then he had to pass a test about his knowledge of English and of American institutions, quite simple a test to be sure, but a test nevertheless, before being naturalized. During World War II Congress changed the rules for those of us in uniform. All we had to do was indicate our intentions of acquiring American passports and a federal judge could swear us in. About half way through training an Army truck took several Mexican citizens, two Italians and me to nearby San Luis Obispo. There we were brought before a judge who looked at the motley crew before him with what seemed to me great distaste.

"Any of you guys speak English?" Three or four of us raised our hand.

"All right. Those of you who can repeat the pledge of allegiance after me." We did so.

"Congratulations. All of you are American citizens now."

"Ya todos somos Norteamericanos." I told the Mexicans. They yelled and clapped. Then we all went back to the camp.

Infantry training was not easy. Since coming to Sacramento I had not participated in any organized athletics. Except for my hunting trips and bicycling to school and back I had led a pretty sedentary life. Suddenly I had to perform push ups by the dozens, go on ten to twenty mile hikes, and partake in various other activities that at least in the first six weeks of army life caused my spoiled body to complain bitterly. Luckily I could shoot well. The two New Yorkers had at least an equally hard time with physical strain; in addition, neither one had ever fired a gun. So as trainees, they were on the bottom of the heap and were made the butt of many jokes and taunted for their lack of military skills, while I was not bothered.

Perhaps also I had learned to adapt quickly to new environments. I made friends with the man the mountaineers seemed to regard as their leader, a man named Baker, or perhaps he chose to make friends with me. He and I became buddies in the army sense. For example, on overnight hikes we shared a tent, or when any exercise required cooperation of two soldiers, he and I worked together. Why he picked me and not one of his camp McQuaide friends I have no idea. Certainly it was not because of my physical abilities; quite frequently he would do more than his share when it came to carrying packs on long hikes or hauling ammunition over difficult terrain. Perhaps he was as curious about me as I was about him. He was appalled at my not having any religion spelled out on my dog tags. "I belong to the Church of Christ," he announced as if this made him something special. But he talked about it as if it were an insurance policy, not a faith. When I said this to him, he produced the special grin I had seen when he played cards and said: "Well? Ain't nothing wrong with that, buddy."

I helped him with paperwork including letters to his family and arranging his government insurance. He was an excellent poker player and, at some expense to me, taught me many of the subtleties of the game. He obviously did not know how to calculate odds of various hands, but had an intuitive grasp of probabilities that was quite amazing. In addition he could maintain the same disarmingly ingenuous smile ("Who me?"} whether he was bluffing or holding a winning hand.

During the last few weeks of basic training, we were assigned tasks more specialized than shooting of rifles and marching in various formations. Baker, several of the others and I were trained to aim and shoot howitzers, clumsy cannons designed to lob shells over hills or other intervening obstacles. Map coordinates, elevation or azimuth angles and muzzle velocities presented no problems to me. To Baker and his followers these were utterly foreign ideas. I spent considerable time with him trying to make those notions seem reasonable. The first few days all I received were blank stares. But something happened in that curious brain of his. All of sudden he could identify coordinates, and correctly call for angular corrections to be applied to the howitzers to zero in on a target. As a result he was certified as having completed howitzer training and this was so noted in his personnel files. Most of his friends were not able to complete the last part of their training. Many years later I received a letter from him, barely legible, in which he suggested that perhaps his howitzer training had saved his life. Assigned to an infantry division, he found himself in a relatively safe cannon company, while most of his cohorts were assigned to rifle companies and many of them were killed in the savage island fighting.

All the men I trained with, including Baker, were sent to fight the Japanese. I, however, was shipped to Europe as an infantry replacement. I suppose it was my ability to speak several languages that made the difference, although GI wisdom would have predicted that the army would send anyone speaking European languages to New Guinea.

I left for Europe in the late spring of 1944. The German U-boats were very active; crossing the Atlantic entailed considerable danger. Most ships moved in large convoys, escorted by destroyers and anti-submarine boats. There was a controversy in the Navy: Should ships capable of high speed be part of a necessarily slow convoy, or would they face less danger if they were to take advantage of their swiftness and perhaps outrun the U-boats? I think the ship on which I sailed was in the nature of an experiment to attempt to decide this controversy. A former liner of the Holland America, it had at one time been a sister ship of the SS Staatendam, the ship that had taken my family to the United States. Its interior had been converted to carry large number of troops, but that did not impair its great speed.

Ships left from various Atlantic ports to make it more difficult for the U-boats to predetermine their paths. We left from a port in Maine in the middle of the night. The ship, with its cargo of soldiers packed more tightly than sardines, went at top speed, without naval protection. On board we heard rumors of submarine sightings, none verified, but actually the voyage was uneventful. There was the expected number of poker games and I mentally thanked Baker for his instruction. While I did not win any money, I did not lose any. My thought had been that our destination would be England, so it was quite a surprise when after a few days the ship somewhat triumphantly steamed through the Straight of Gibraltar into the Mediterranean and then docked at Naples.

I spent two nights in what the GI's called a repl depot; a tent city where newly arrived soldiers were housed until assigned to replace those killed or wounded in combat. Infantry men were most in demand, casualties among them were highest, and I was rapidly assigned to the Third Infantry Division, a Regular Army Division that had seen much combat in North Africa and now was fighting in Italy. In it the life expectancy of a green infantry replacement was considerably less than three score and ten. But I was lucky. Because In California I had trained with howitzers, I saw service in the somewhat sheltered bosom of a regimental cannon company, as apparently had my buddy, Baker. Within a week of my arrival in Europe I was promoted to the exalted status of Private First Class.

1944: Dangerous Mission.

After only a few weeks of combat, I was ordered by one of the company officers to report to regimental headquarter. I asked him what it as all about, but he said he had no idea. A jeep that had earlier brought some supplies from headquarters deposited me at a tent some five miles away from the company bivouac.

"PFC Hahn reporting," I told a sergeant who was sitting behind a table in a tent that had a sign over its flap that said: Regimental HQ.

"What the hell do you want?" He acted as though he had never heard of me nor had any idea why I might have been asked to report.

"I really don't know. I am only obeying orders."

"Who the fuck told you to come here?"

"Lt. Bernovsky, the exec officer of cannon company."

"Well shit, you better go back and ask this thirty- day wonder what the hell you are supposed to do here." He turned his back to me and returned to his paperwork.

"Any body else might know why I was asked to report here?"

"You can always ask the colonel." Sure, and get my ass chewed out royally. I didn't know what to do and was already leaving, when the sergeant turned around and yelled after me:

"What the hell did your say your name was?"

I repeated it.

"Well, maybe you are one of the clowns that's supposed to see this civilian creep that's been hanging around. Wait and I'll check with Captain O'Leary." He twisted a crank on his battery operated phone spoke a few words that I did not hear. He yawned at me

"Yeah, that's it. The Captain will be over to take you to see this clown."

A captain will be over to take a lowly private to see a civilian in a war zone? I acutely resented the artificial barrier the army threw up between officers and enlisted men. What's going on around here? I wondered. Probably this sergeant is pulling my leg, I thought. The noise in the tent made me aware of the rain that had begun to fall and I could hear the now familiar sound of cannon fire in the distance. Luckily I had worn my field jacket because it had been unusually cold in the morning. The sergeant had closed the tent flap to keep out the water that now came tumbling from the dark cloud cover. I had taken off my helmet, but the sergeant snapped at me:

"Put that back on, soldier. Orders from the colonel. We are to wear helmets at all times." Indeed, he was wearing his.

I had heard about this colonel who issued all sorts of orders that most soldiers considered to be chickenshit, so I put my heavy headgear back on. It was only a few minutes later that the flap opened and a captain came into the tent. He wore paratroopers' boots and his paratrooper insignias were sewn on his shirt. His helmet was dripping with water. His movements were graceful and athletic, like those of a big cat.

"Boy, it's wet out there." The sergeant and I stood at attention. "At ease."

He whirled around and looked at me. "You Hahn?" Not Private Hahn, but Hahn.

"Yes sir."

"Good. Follow me."

I put on my jacket and went out into the rain.

The Captain, in spite of his earlier complaint, did not seem to mind the weather. He walked next to me, very quickly, and started asking me questions in rapid, excellent German. Where was I born, how well did I remember Vienna, how did I feel about the Nazis. I answered, also in German. The questions came in a swift staccato like bullets from a machinegun, so fast that I did not have time to wonder why a Captain O'Leary was speaking German and asking me curious questions. It was then my impression that he was more interested in whether I understood him and in the manner of my answers then in the content of my responses.

We came to another tent and he quickly pulled back its flap and equally quickly pulled it shut after we had entered. He seemed unable to move slowly. I don't remember his face or his height or the color of his hair, only his hyperactive movements remain in my memory. Rain dripped from my helmet and my jacket, but neither the Captain nor the other man in the room paid the slightest attention.

"Joe, this guy's German is just fine."

'Joe' was walking around the room smoking a cigarette. He was a short, rather thin, sandy haired but with thick eyebrows that seemed to twitch continuously. His other motions, however, had none of the lithe, hyper quality that characterized those of the paratrooper. While 'Joe' was wearing an Army officer's uniform, it had no insignia to tell me what organization he represented nor indication of rank to tell me how to address him. 'This must be the civilian creep the sergeant had mentioned', I thought to myself.

The civilian turned to me. "If the Captain says you can speak German, you can speak it. So many guys claim to speak the language but when you listen to them they sound like freshmen in a foreign language class. I am Joe Green, by the way." He stuck out his hand.

"Private Hahn." I did not know if I should salute, but since his hand was invitingly extended, I just shook it.

Now Green sat down at a table and began looking at a stack of papers in front of him. He started to ask me questions, mainly about Germany, German politics, the Wehrmacht. Did I now who Rommel was? Kesselring? Von Kleist? The questions were put rather slowly, in almost a schoolmaster's fashion. I had followed the war pretty closely so I had no problem in identifying these German generals. But I grew tired of what seemed to me to be a strange game of questions and answers.

"What's this all about, Sir? Why are you asking me all these questions?"

"Look." He was not slow about responding. "It must be obvious to you that we are here for a purpose. If you don't want to answer any more questions, that's fine. We will just send you back to your unit and nobody will be any wiser, and nobody will hold it against you. I, however, would suggest that you humor us for a while".

The captain, who had been pacing around the room watching me, I thought, as a predator might observe his potential prey, broke in:

"You made it pretty damn clear to me that you don't care for the Nazis. Now you might have a chance of really doing something about that." It seemed that he had listened to my answers to his questions after all.

"Well, why not. I have always liked Twenty Questions." I was getting quite scared about what was going on and, perhaps to overcome my fear, had to make some smart-alecky comment.

Green, if that really was his name, just smiled but the paratrooper added, somewhat sharply: "I can god damn well assure you we are not playing games here."

For about another hour I answered questions. At first these once more tested my knowledge about the current German scene: did I know about the various party organizations, could I distinguish

137

the SS from the SA, what is the function of the Gestapo, is food rationed in Germany, had I ever heard of the Abwehr, the German Army intelligence service and so on. My answers to these must have satisfied the questioner because he proceeded to a different subject.

Did I know anything about electrical devices, about radios, mechanical devices? I told him about pinball machines and overhead cranes. Finally he wanted to know how I felt about Communism, did I admire Stalin, the Russians, did I think the Negroes in the US were oppressed, was I happy that I had gone to the US, did I plan to stay there after the war, why did I enter the Army when I could have avoided service. Apparently my responses to these last questions convinced him of what really was the truth, namely that I was not a Stalinist and that I had become a staunch American Chauvinist delighted to have received my citizenship.

The captain, from behind me, said something to the civilian that sounded like "Sounds OK to me". Green his head.

"I have one more question for you, George." It was the first time he had used my first name. "Would you be willing to volunteer for a job that might entail considerable danger?" He anticipated my question. "I can't tell you much about it. It will involve more training and may prevent you from contacting your family for some time."

By now I would have had to be an imbecile not to realize that I was being vetted for some type of intelligence operation. I was certainly frightened and I remembered a cardinal rule among enlisted men in the Army: Never volunteer for anything! But as far as danger was concerned, I told myself that being in combat in the infantry, even in the cannon company, was not exactly a sinecure. And the thought of being a member of some secret, perhaps important, anti-Nazi operation excited me to the point that I began to shake! I had visions of being a commando, silently killing SS men and liberating Gestapo prisoners, and above all of revenge for the deaths of so many members of my family. It did not take me long to decide to volunteer.

"Be sure about this. Later it will be difficult to change your mind." The civilian smiled at me. "Let's see if there is any coffee in the officers' mess, and, if you still want to volunteer when we get back, we have authority to cut your orders immediately."

"Put on your field jacket." The captain slapped me on the back. "No one needs to see that PFC stripe. We'll go to the officers' mess, and the folks there are pretty gung-ho about sticking to rules.

No enlisted men in the officers' mess. If there is a problem, just say that I ordered you to accompany us." Again the artificial difference made between enlisted men and officers was rubbed in my face. But that day Private Hahn had coffee in the officer's mess. The coffee, however, did not taste much better than the usual GI brew.

"So, change your mind?" Back at the tent where I had answered the myriad of questions, the paratrooper wanted to know.

"No, sir. Definitely not."

"Good. I have a jeep from the HQ. motor pool. I'll take you to your unit and you can get your stuff. In the meantime Joe can get your orders cut. You'll stay here overnight and tomorrow morning you can go to Naples on the mail plane. From there ATS, the Army Transport Service, can fly you to England." To England!

Getting my stuff was not quite as easy as the captain had thought. My company commander objected strenuously to my leaving. He and the paratrooper almost got into an argument.

"My company is already short of experienced men. Most of these replacements I get don't know their ass from a hole in the ground. Here I finally get one who seems to understand these weapons and then the fucking crazy army wants to transfer him out. Hell of a way to run a war!" Finally, the company commander contacted regimental HQ. He then turned to me.

"Nothing I can do, I guess. Get your crap together and get the hell out of here." I must admit it was music to my ears to hear these officers almost fight over me. All my crap easily fitted into one duffel bag and I was ready to leave within minutes. That night I slept in a tent at regimental HQ.

The next morning I was handed my orders. They didn't read PFC Hahn but S/A Hahn, CIC, att. 2568 WDD. Overnight I had become a Special Agent in the Army Counter Intelligence Corps. It was not difficult to figure out that att. meant attached, but I had no idea what WDD stood for. I asked the sergeant who handed me my papers.

"How the shit should I know!" He was not too helpful.

That morning I saw neither the paratrooper nor the civilian. At six, it was just turning light, I went to the little airstrip where the mail plane landed daily at sundown and took off in the morning after Allied planes had cleared the skies of German fighters. It was a small plane that, in addition to the pilot, could only hold three passengers. There were already three officers waiting two Majors and a First Lieutenant. I assumed that I was on the bottom of the pecking order and would have to wait until the next day. The pilot looked at all our orders.

"Sorry," he said to the lieutenant, "this guy," pointing at me, "has orders that have higher priority than yours. You will have to wait till tomorrow." The lieutenant glared at my PFC stripe. I felt as though the beautiful princess had kissed me.

In Naples I caught a transport plane to Dakar, and from there to an air base near Manchester, where, in a hangar that served as reception area, I found a desk that sported a sign that said: 'All enlisted personnel must report here'. The air force non-com who manned the desk looked at my orders and eyed me curiously and somewhat suspiciously.

"Over there, sir." He pointed at a desk that had a different sign: 'Officers and US Civilians on Military Orders'.

I took my orders to that desk. Another non-com took one look at my PFC stripe and barked: "Can't you read, soldier? Over there." He pointed at the desk that I had just left. Not only did I wear PFC stripes but also I did not look much older than my eighteen years. Furthermore I was unshaven, my hair was a mess and my uniform was still full of Italian mud. But somehow, magically it seemed to me, I had been placed on the other side of the officer-enlisted men barrier. I must admit that I was quick to take advantage of this

"Can't you read, corporal? Take a look at my orders".

The soldier gave me a fishy look, but did read my papers.

"Sorry, sir, but your uniform..."

He consulted a list tacked onto his desk. "The army bus does not go by your outfit. I'll notify them that you are here. According to my info, they will provide you with transport. Please wait over there, sir." Now he was careful to address me by my newly acquired title. He pointed at some benches.

About twenty minutes later a young woman sporting the uniform of the women's auxiliary corps, a WAC, came into the hangar, spoke to the corporal at the desk and then came to me.

"Mr. Hahn?" She also looked with curiosity at the lone stripe on my dirty, lowly uniform. "I will take you to the detachment." I grabbed my duffel bag and followed her.

The jeep she drove had neatly stenciled black 2568 WDD markings on its white bumper. I still had no idea what WDD stood for and I was too embarrassed to ask the WAC. The ride took about 15 minutes during which I tried to make conversation with her, but she did not seem very keen on talking to me. We arrived at what seemed to me to be a country manor. The large, two wings, two-story house was built of stone, with Ivy climbing many of the walls. Extensive lawns surrounded it, with a neglected flower garden in the center of a circular driveway. Had it not been for the several jeeps and even a Ford sedan that were parked near the front entrance, it could have served as a movie setting for a Jane Austin novel. All had the vehicles had same markings: 2568 WDD.

The WAC parked her jeep, I grabbed my bag, and she and I walked into the house. To my right I saw a large room with easy chairs, tables, bookshelves and people reading books. Books! I hadn't seen anybody read anything except the Stars And Stripes, the daily US Army paper, since I had arrived in Europe. Some of the readers were in civilian clothes, but most wore the same uniform Green had worn. A few of them had paratrooper wings displayed on their shirts or jackets, the only insignia of any kind that I saw.

"The office is over there". The WAC pointed along the hall that was on our left. "The guys on duty will take care of you. They are expecting you." I took my bag, walked along the hall until I came to a room that was stenciled with: "Orderly room, 2568 War Department Det." So now I knew what WDD stood for, but I wasn't any wiser about its function.

The orderly room was perhaps the only part of this country house that maintained a semblance of military appearance. On a wall I saw that duty rosters were posted. File cabinets were painted olive drab, and each carried a sign: 'Must be kept locked'. The two desks carried 'In' and 'Out' baskets like all orderly room desks in the army. One desk had a sign identifying its occupant as duty sergeant although the individual sitting behind it wore an officer's uniform devoid of rank insignia. I did not know how to identify myself, so I decided to play it safe and reported as PFC Hahn.

The sergeant, if that is what he was, grinned and yelled to another man wearing the same information-less uniform: "Hey, Anton, here I thought you were getting a hot shot CIC agent and instead here comes this PFC. And if his looks reflect his age, we are robbing the cradle these days." The man had a point. As I looked around, then and later, it seemed that I was younger by several years than any other member of the detachment. He turned to me. "Kid, never mind my bullshit. Anyway this is the last time for quite a while that you will want to tell your rank. As far as anybody here, or for that matter anywhere else, is concerned, you are Special

141

Agent Hahn and you will be addressed as Mr. Hahn. And get rid of that filthy uniform. I'll have the supply room issue you a set of officers' greens. That's what everybody around here wears. You'll soon notice that this is a funny outfit. The usual army rules don't mean shit around here."

"As you know, I was just attached to this outfit. What the hell is going on here?"

"Have you talked to Mr. Dodge? He's the Commanding Officer. You'll have to hear it from him. But let me fix you up with a place to sleep. And get you some clothes."

Turning to the other man in the room. "Hey, Anton, take our new friend here upstairs. Have him share a room with Bill Horton, he is all by himself. And then for chrissake get him some decent clothes. He looks like a soldier, and we can't have any of that around here."

I had a night in a real bed, after a shower and shave, in a room I had all to myself. Mr. Horton, it seemed was 'away'. As I found out soon enough, people seemed to be 'away' a lot from the detachment. In the morning, I had been outfitted with a set of greens and although my boots did not fit too well, I looked almost human when I had my appointment with Mr.Dodge. He was a man perhaps in his fifties, dressed in the same insignia-less uniform that nearly everybody else wore. But he walked erect and exuded a military air that belied the civilian aspect of his attire. Although there was a desk in his sparsely furnished office, he stood or walked around the room for most of my interview. His blond hair was beginning to thin, perhaps even to gray, but his bright blue, darting eyes gave his face an attractive youthfulness. He was easily as tall as I was, a little over 6 feet, and his clipped voice had an accent that I assumed to be New England.

He did not waste many words. I would have to take some tests and if I passed them, then I would get additional training. Only after I had finished that could he talk to me about my assignment.

"You are a radio expert, I have been told."

I demurred saying that while I did know something about electrical circuits, I knew very little about radios, except what I had learned in High School. He sighed.

"Well, that's the civilian army. We requested a communications expert and they send us a school boy." Dodge was a West Point man, as I found out later.

He looked at me sharply: "Do you know the difference between a diode and a triode?" That much I did know and described the difference between the two types of vacuum tubes.

"And what's the function of the third terminal in the triode?"

"It controls the amplification."

"At least you know that much. I suppose you can learn the rest. It says in your files that your German is flawless. I am no judge of that, but for your own sake, if you have any doubts about that, if you don't think you can pass as a German, tell me now."

"My German is OK, sir. I can pass as an Austrian or Bavarian but not as a northerner or Berliner."

"That's OK. In fact that's good. By the way, you are not supposed to "sir" me. That's against our rules. We don't want any outsiders to know who is who around here."

He looked at me again. "You look like you are in reasonable physical shape. You think you can stand up under a few weeks of pretty strenuous training?"

"Yes, sir. Yes, Mr. Dodge, I mean."

That was about the extent of my first interview with Mr. Dodge. During the next week I was subjected to a variety of tests that were supposed to determine my fitness for intelligence work. I must have passed them, because I then was sent to a British training center where I learned, among other things, how to operate and repair radio sets.

At the camp I was treated as an officer. My roommate was a British lieutenant whose major topic of conversation was sex. He regaled me with stories about his conquests and went into details about the physical aspects of his romances. My own sexual experience was extremely limited, but I matched his tales readily. I had read enough pornography to enable me to sound convincing. He was very curious about my title, Special Agent, and asked all kinds of questions. I repeatedly had to tell him that I was not allowed to go into details.

We learned how to disable opponents, cut throats, use our knees to squash the sexual organs of enemies. Our instructors kept repeating over and over again: "Forget the Marquis of Queensbury rules. Use any way you can to kill your enemy."

They taught us how to fold parachutes. And how to jump out of airplanes.

"If this is your first jump, plug up your bunghole with paper," the British jump sergeant warned us. And I realized what he meant when that jump door opened and I felt the cold blast of air hitting my face and I looked out into what seemed to be nothingness. Others have told me that they were thrilled and excited by their first jump; I was only scared.

After I finished the training, I returned to the 'Country House', that's what most of its tenants called it, hoping that now I could start my assignment. By this time it was mid-July of 1944. I had learned enough about the War Department Detachments to realize that these were cover names for units set up for specific intelligence purposes and under the overall jurisdiction of the Office of Strategic Services, the forerunner of the CIA.

Mr. Dodge was 'away'; Anton, who apparently was my superior, although nobody had told me, gave me the task of translating some German documents that dealt with the organization of the Nazi security services, complete with names of the officials occupying various slots. The papers were stamped "Top Secret", so I knew I had truly become a member of the intelligence community. I took my first task very seriously and completed the rendering of the papers into English in one marathon twelve-hour session. When I returned them to my boss, he smiled and told me not to let on to others that I could translate that quickly, or I would find myself exclusively shuffling papers. I didn't tell him how many hours I had actually spent doing the work.

I had not written to my family nor heard from them in weeks. I could not tell them about my present status, nor was I sure that I was permitted to contact them. I was too bashful to ask anyone. Somehow Dodge's calling me a schoolboy had become known and I was frequently so addressed. I did not want to appear too juvenile, so I asked a minimum of questions.

The news about the abortive attempt on Hitler's life late in July stuck Country House like a tornado. Not only did it become the main topic of conversation, but also it seemed to me that many of the individuals at 'Country House' had been aware of the assassination plan. I heard that Admiral Canaris, the head of the German Army counter intelligence operations, an active participant in the plot, had been in touch with American Intelligence in Switzerland. Now the Gestapo had arrested him, and everybody expected Hitler to exact bloody revenge.

Dodge returned early in August. He talked to me a few days later. I was not particularly surprised by what he told me. My mission was no longer of interest to the detachment. Although he did not say so, I had gathered from comments Anton and others had made, that it had been associated with the attempt on Hitler's life and its hoped for aftermath, a quick surrender by the Germans to the Western Allies. Now I was to be reassigned to an operational CIC detachment, but first loaned to another unit, also under OSS control, now in France, that needed an agent who could speak both French and German. French wasn't exactly my native tongue; mine was rather of the classroom variety, and I told this to Dodge. He just shrugged.

"There is nobody else available. I think you'll do just fine."

I wondered, since he knew practically nothing about me, how he could come to this conclusion. By now I knew better than to ask him what my job would be. He probably didn't know, but if he did, he would not tell me. I expected that I would now become involved in some direct anti-German activity. Life at the country house was certainly pleasant, but hardly fulfilled my heroic visions of killing SS men and Gestapo torturers.

Within days of my conversation with Dodge, I found myself transferred to detachment operating on the Spanish-French frontier. When I arrived, I was greeted with considerable anticipation.

"We really need somebody fluent in French and Spanish. Glad to have you."

I had considerable doubt about my fluency in French. About that in Spanish I had none. It was nonexistent. When I told that to the 'civilian' in charge of the unit, he acted, at least initially, as though I had perpetrated the fraud of the century. I didn't think that I was to blame, nor did I think the civilian army bore any responsibility.

"Even the vaunted OSS can foul up", I thought to myself.

Again I was left without an assignment; worse, I was clearly an outsider in this small, tightly knit group. Most of the individuals in the detachment were graduates from Ivy League schools and they had been together for well over a year. They were not interested in talking to a young kid who had not been to any college. I only got to know one individual, who was a stranger like myself. This was a young Free French lieutenant who was assigned as liaison to the Americans. He was treated with suspicion by the OSS agents, at least so he felt, and thought that he was wasting his time,

"Do they think that I am a German spy?" He asked me. That was almost how I felt about their treatment of me. His English was about on the same level as my French. We would talk in French until I encountered a word or phrase that I knew only in English then I would switch to that language. English would last until the lieutenant, out of similar necessity, switched back to French. In this way we got along just fine, and his English and my French improved considerably.

He had a jeep assigned to him, and he and I drove it all over the liberated areas of Western France; we even went to Paris after Leclerc's French divisions had freed it. We were often stopped by military police who were quite frequently baffled by our papers. We learned quickly that if the police were American, the Free French papers worked best, while at both British and French checkpoints my American CIC identification was least likely to be questioned.

It did not take me very long to realize that if I stayed in the OSS detachment I might well spend the rest of the war enjoying the French countryside, but I would have no chance of fulfilling my fantasies of anti Nazi heroism. So I requested a transfer to a line CIC team. One of these was attached to each army division and I knew that German speaking agents were in considerable demand. The head of the OSS detachment raised no objections, and my transfer to a divisional CIC team came just in time for the last major German counteroffensive that led to the Battle of the Bulge. It was the last gasp of the once invincible Wehrmacht. Rumors were circulating that, as part of the attack, Germans in American uniforms were infiltrating US lines, supposedly with orders to assassinate General Eisenhower.

The German offensive, begun Dec 16, caught Allied troops by surprise. The Germans overran American positions; almost eight thousand surrendered to the advancing Nazis, while many more fled in panic. Near Strasbourg, captured by Devers' Sixth Army Group only three weeks earlier, the roads were jammed with fleeing GI's. Many of these were stragglers separated from their units, a situation tailor-made for infiltrating spies and assassins. Roadblocks, manned primarily by military policemen were set up on all roads. Soldiers passing these and not moving as part of organized units were detained by the policemen and then interrogated by military and counter intelligence agents.

So, as my first real CIC assignment, I spent countless hours questioning GI's:

"Who won the last World Series?" "How many homeruns did Babe Ruth hit in his last year with the Yankees?" These were the kind of questions I, an eighteen year old kid who spoke with a slight German accent, who knew next to nothing about professional

146

baseball, asked veteran US soldiers over and over again. The irony hardly escaped me. At times I felt that my involvement with the intelligence community had turned into an absurd joke. I did not find any spies or saboteurs and began to believe that I would never have the chance to use my recently acquired skills to effect at least some level of revenge against SS and Gestapo personnel.

Perhaps because of my frequent changes in assignments I had not been promoted. I was still a PFC, and on private's pay. An Army snafu prevented me from getting my paratroop allowance. Yet I lived in officers' quarters, wore officers' uniforms and was instructed to keep my rank, or rather lack of rank, a secret.

"I am not being outranked here," was the phrase I was instructed to use if anyone had the temerity to question my status.

I had not heard from my family in months. My repeated changes of address prevented mail from catching up with me. I also had not written home in some time. I had signed a secrecy oath, and I was confused about what I was allowed to write and what was forbidden. My parents, especially my mother, would have been terrified at the thought of my going through paratroop training and so I took the easy way out and did not write. I found out later that Father had written to the commanding general of the 3rd Infantry Division asking about me 'even if the news is bad'. I knew he had changed jobs recently, working as an estimator for a construction company; Mother had also changed jobs. Now she was working for a wholesale butcher. My sister Lucie had moved to Berkeley where she was attending the University of California. I frequently wondered how they were all getting along in their new environments. But not enough to write.

Curiously, in Europe I heard much less about the fate of European Jewry than I had in Sacramento. The Army newspaper hardly ever mentioned these millions. The OSS and CIC agents did not seem interested in the horrors that were going on in all of Nazi occupied Europe. It was as if the Jews, Gypsies, Poles and other victims of organized mass murder never existed. I was repeatedly overwhelmed by the thought that the world just did not give a damn or simply ascribed all the reports to propaganda.

It was only after the defeat of the last German offensive, after the Allied troops moved deeply into Germany and camp after camp was liberated, that the extent of German mass murder and torture could no longer be attributed to Jewish fabrication. Stories showing graphic pictures of unbelievable bestiality and eyewitness accounts of the liberation of concentration camps now appeared regularly in the Stars and Stripes, the Army newspaper. By then I was, at least to some extent, finally involved in the kind of intelligence work that I had envisaged initially when I volunteered for a 'dangerous mission'.

1945: Supermen.

I became involved in he interrogation of Germans suspected of having belonged to the SS or the Gestapo. What kind of people were they? Supermen? I remember one of my early suspects. I tried to put myself into his shoes.

The coal furnace was going full blast even though it was August and outside the sun was shining. In spite of the heat, the prisoner's teeth were chattering. He had been ordered to take off all his clothes, but had kept his underpants on nevertheless. His ribs were showing through his skin that appeared yellow in the harsh, bright light given off by the overhead bulb. Occasionally he ran his hands through his sandy hair in a nervous, jerky motion. He sat on the small stool in front of a large desk. It, and the two empty chairs behind it, were the only pieces of furniture in the concrete lined chamber. He could see only one door, not far from the desk.

"I won't tell them anything," he thought to himself. "They probably don't know much about me anyway. If they ask me about my co-workers, I'll invent some names. But I won't tell them what they want to know."

The prisoner's eyes periodically darted across the room. He did not want to look at the two enormous men who had come into the room recently and were now standing near the large furnace, but he seemed unable to avoid staring in their direction. They were taking off their shirts and their skin glistened with sweat. His eyes seemed to fasten on their impressive arm and chest muscles. He looked at his own. They seemed puny by comparison and he began to feel very vulnerable. The men were talking to each other, occasionally laughing, They paid no attention to the prisoner.

He knew their type only too well, though, from past prison experiences. Probably they were sadists who enjoyed the pain they inflicted on their victims. He noticed a wooden club that momentarily rested at the feet of one of the brutes. Occasionally the two giants kicked it back and forth between them, as if it were a football. It made a clattering noise as it rolled on the stone floor. The prisoner could already imagine the different noise his bones would make as the club was swung against his limbs.

The chair behind the desk was still empty. The prisoner's panic increased. He did not know whether he wanted his interrogation to start or if he was glad for the few extra minutes of pain free existence.

"It's the knee cap that hurts most. When they bust your kneecap, the pain can become unbearable. Then there are no more secrets". He could not remember who had told him that. One of his colleagues most likely. Perhaps it wasn't even true. There might even be worse pains. His eyes returned to the muscles of the men by the furnace. In his mind he could already see the club hitting his leg. How well he knew the routine. One would be holding him, while the other would be methodically using the club to break his bones. Which of these monsters would be swinging it? He tried to tell by looking at their faces, but their expressions gave him no clue.

Now he started to find it difficult to breathe. Fear appeared to constrict his throat and chest. "Why don't they start?" His earlier bravado was now forgotten. "Perhaps if I give them a few names they will be satisfied." He remembered one prisoner, a young man who claimed not to be involved in any anti occupation activity. He was foolish, or perhaps really innocent, and refused to name names. The beating that followed had been merciless. A record player had been blaring away to drown out the victim's shrieks. After what seemed a long time the young man suddenly stopped screaming and collapsed. He could not be revived even when buckets of ice cold water were thrown at him. As he was dragged from the room, he appeared to be lifeless.

The prisoner looked around the room for a record player. He did not see one, but there was a box on the desk. Perhaps it was hidden there. He began to cry, first quietly, then sobbing loudly. One of the giants heard him, briefly looked at him, and then said something to his partner. They both laughed loudly.

As he remembered more and more interrogation horrors, the prisoner's resolve to only "give them a few names" dissolved more and more. "Why should I die?" he asked himself. "There is no point to it now." His sobbing grew louder.

He was losing all sense of time. He tried to make himself think of events not related to his present state, tried to think of the last time he had been with a woman, the last good meal he had had, but nothing worked. He could not overcome his panic, could not stop crying.

On the other side of the door that the prisoner had seen, two men were seated at a table. They were wearing dark green uniforms, officers' shirts and pants but no jackets or ties, without indications of rank. The only breaks in the monotony of their attire were two small brass US insignias affixed to the ends of the collars of their shirts and the paratrooper wings they both sported. Sheets of papers from a manila folder were scattered on the table and the men were reading the typed pages. Occasionally one or the other would make a note on a pad of paper that sat half way between them.

"Well, I suppose we know enough about this fucking bastard." One of the men, he was the older one, all of twenty-five, began to gather all the papers. "Besides he has probably sweated enough. By now the cocksucker ought to be so scared that he should be ready to sell his mother."

The other American, not much more than a boy, nodded his head. "I am always amazed when these swine start ratting on their comrades. The great supermen. This one seems to be as vile as they come. Did you read the affidavit from the Polish captain?"

"You mean about the fucking bone breaking routine they used in Krakow? All these shit eating Gestapo teams used torture. But this syphilitic piece of crap in there apparently enjoyed watching. Another affidavit talks about a session where one of the prisoners had his balls crushed. And this sweetie watched all the time, grinning. Now the prick can think of all the things we'll do to him. Sometimes I am sorry that it's only a fucking show and that we don't really beat them up. You know, kid, that's why they talk so easily. They think the rest of the world behaves the same way they did."

He took the pad with all the notes. "We'll do the usual routine. I'll act as though I did not know any German. You 'interpret'. I'll yell and scream until he pisses blood. Then you can rub lard on his ass to make him feel good. The fucker, he'll love you so much he'll tell you all his secrets."

They entered the furnace room. The two giants, one of them black, waved at them, while the prisoner quickly rose from his chair and stood at attention. The kid had never seen the prisoner, but had imagined him as a blond giant, a superman of the Goebbels propaganda machine. Instead he saw a small, ordinary looking man, almost pathetic as he stood in his dirty underpants. Although he had stopped crying, his whole body expressed fear. Had the kid not read the man's dossier, he might have felt sorry for him. "How could I ever have thought of the Nazis as supermen?" he thought to himself.

"You were told to take off all your goddamn clothes. Take off those fucking underpants". In translation, the kid omitted the swearwords.

"But sir..." The prisoner tried to use his few words of English.

"Don't sir me, you disgusting piece of garbage. Just take off the pants." The interrogator knew that few things make a man feel more vulnerable than losing the protection offered by his clothes.

"I...I have the...the Geschlechts Krankheit." The prisoner started to cry again.

"So our whoremonger has the clap! I don't give a shit if you are a leper and your prick is about to fall off, take off those fucking underpants." Even when the obscenities were omitted the threatening tone was obvious. The prisoner took off his undergarment and now looked even more pathetic with his penis wrapped in what appeared to have been a white handkerchief. He placed his hands over his genitals as if he wanted to provide some cover against his interrogators' stares.

The questioning now proceeded rapidly. Name, age, birthplace etc. were quickly verified. The prisoner regained control of himself and stopped crying. Asked for his profession, he said, "Personnel clerk".

"When did you become a member of the National Socialist Party?"

"1932" So he was a party member even before the Nazis came to power in Germany.

"Were you ever a member of the SA?"

"No."

"The SS?"

"Yes."

"The Gestapo?"

Hesitation. "Yes."

"What was your function?"

More hesitation. "I was in charge of personnel files."

The interrogator motioned to the two men who slowly walked to the prisoner's side. The kid leaned over the desk and very quietly said to the shivering man: "I would strongly advise you not to lie. We already have a lot of information about you. My colleague has a terrible temper and, if provoked, there is no telling what he might do. I don't want to see you get hurt, so be careful".

The older man picked up the cue: "If I believed you piss drinking bastards I would have to think that the Gestapo was just one big, friendly personnel department." His voice rose threateningly. "If I catch you lying again...." One of the big men picked up his bat and looked at the prisoner.

"Sir, I was in charge of personnel in Krakow from 1940 to 1941. I didn't lie." The kid thought the prisoner was going to cry again, but he didn't although he was shaking visibly.

"And after that?"

"I was attached to an interrogation team."

"What the hell do you mean by 'attached' you stinking weasel?"

"I had to attend interrogations of Communists."

"We have three sworn statements from members of one of the Krakow Gestapo teams that you were its commanding officer at least from 1942 until you ran when the Russians were coming. Is that what you mean by attending, you sickening excuse for a human being?"

The kid leaned over the table again and almost whispered: "I won't be able to warn you again. I am really trying to help you, but if you don't cooperate..." He shook his head and glanced at the big men.

The Gestapo man's eyes now focused on the size of the bat. He turned to the kid. "If these men will go away I'll tell you what you want to know."

The men withdrew and the man admitted his role, described the team, gave names and told of Polish Army officers, of civilians and Russian prisoners of war that had been tortured and killed.

"It was wartime. Whatever we did we did for our country."

"Twenty, fifty years from now your country won't thank you for disgracing it like that." He turned to me. "I better leave before I kill this stinking bastard."

The older man walked out of the room. The Gestapo officer rapidly put on his underpants. The kid opened a pack of cigarettes and offered one to the prisoner, who quickly accepted it and the light provided.

The kid said in an almost friendly tone: "You know that you will now be transferred to an internment camp. You are on the Polish war crimes list, and you will then be turned over to them."

"They will kill me."

"Well, perhaps we can work out something. You must know other Gestapo agents that live or are in hiding in town. You bring them to our office upstairs here, or tell us where we can find them. One a week and we won't send you to the camp. Don't try to run away, we'll be watching you."

The man breathed deeply, sighed but did not answer.

"If you don't agree, I won't be able to help you. You know, I am supposed to notify the Polish liaison officer in Frankfurt of your arrest. I may have to do that right away."

The prisoner sighed. "If I give you names, no one will know?"

"No one."

"I can't. I would be betraying my friends."

"And you think they did not betray you? How do you think we knew where to find you?"

He sighed again. "I have heard that you have a new drug that can cure my disease. You provide me with that and I'll give you the names you want."

Penicillin was not available. But the kid did obtain sulfa drugs from a local army hospital. And so for six weeks the Gestapo man brought in one name a week. Each led to an arrest of a low level Gestapo agent. The seventh week he could no longer produce a new name. So we shipped him off to the internment camp.

1946;1964: The Children.

In May of 1946 the Army transferred me from Berlin, where I had been stationed since the1945 Potsdam Conference that brought together Truman, Churchill, and Stalin, to the old city of Bremen. Allied bombardments had severely damaged the town. Perhaps 80-90 percent of its houses had been destroyed or made uninhabitable. After my year in Berlin, however, ruined cities no longer impressed me.

Germany then was still divided into four occupation zones. Bremen and its harbor, Bremerhaven, were in an enclave in the British zone administered and governed by the US. Without Bremen, the land-locked American zone would not have had access to the sea.

I was by now a veteran US counter intelligence agent. When the war ended, most of the corps' experienced agents returned to civilian life as soon as possible. Those few of us with one or two years' practice became veterans by default. My primary job was still to trace and arrest Gestapo personnel and individuals on various countries' war crimes lists, though countering Soviet espionage became more and more important. Working for me were three Germans with proven anti-Nazi records, and a Lithuanian whose anti- Nazi credentials were not quite as unimpeachable. The five of us sifted police records, questioned possible informants, read transcripts of war crimes trials, and occasionally, following a tip, arrested and interrogated a suspect. Most of these were low level Gestapo agents or SS officers.

Almost every day an excited informant would tell us of a high ranking Nazi hiding somewhere within our jurisdiction. We investigated all these reports; never did they turn out to be correct. The man most wanted by all Allied intelligence agencies then was Martin Borman, Hitler's deputy. Hardly a week went by that we did not hear of a man who "exactly" matched his description and who was hiding in some ruin of the city. Usually it turned out to be some homeless vagrant who did not resemble Borman in the least. To this day Borman has not been arrested.

One evening, it was perhaps eight o'clock and I was playing poker with several of the other agents, Joachim, one of my German associates, came into the lounge to see me. This was quite unusual. In order not to make their affiliation too obvious, the

Germans were under orders not to enter American quarters except in an emergency.

"Mr. Hahn ", all counter intelligence agents regardless of rank were addressed as Mister, "I think that Fritz Freireich is at his sister's house." Joachim was very excited.

Freireich was a fairly high Gestapo official who had a sordid history of torturing captured members of the French resistance. He was prominent on the French war crimes list. We knew that his sister lived in Bremen and periodically watched her house, hoping that he would make an appearance. I was particularly interested in this man. In his dossier, I had seen a report that Freireich had violated an agreement made in a French provincial town. There the mayor had agreed to instruct his policemen to arrest all local Jewish adults; children, however, were to be allowed to remain in the local orphanage. After the arrest of the adults and their removal to concentration camps, Freireich had ordered his Gestapo agents to raid the orphanage. All the Jewish children were carried off to their death. That report resonated in my memory. It was as if my nightmares had played out in reality.

At first, though, I was not intrigued. "One of your informants' reports, I suppose?"

"It was initially, but I went out to look for myself. The man at his sister's house clearly fits the description that we have." Joachim was very reliable; if he had seen the man, he might well be Freireich.

Now I was becoming excited. I quickly excused myself from the poker game.

"If it is really our man, he is probably armed and we might need help from the military police." We had a direct phone line to the local detachment. Within ten minutes a jeep with five armed Military Policemen was waiting in front of our quarters. Joachim and I took my vehicle and we drove to the edge of the city where Freireich's sister lived. The MP's followed us. I asked three of the policeman to cover the back of the house while the rest of us went to the front door. I knocked. After a minute or so, a woman answered. When we asked about Fritz, she simply said.

" He is upstairs. I know you want him. You won't hurt him will you?" She stood as if to block entrance to the house.

Just then we heard a commotion in the back. Within a few minutes the three policemen who had been at the backdoor came through the house bringing with them a man who walked with a slight but noticeable limp. He had his hands raised above his head. When we got a close look at him, it certainly appeared to be Fritz Freireich: about thirty years old, h brown hair, blue eyes, medium height. The limp was also consistent with his description.

"This clown tried to run away. And he had a gun." One of the policemen gave me the Luger that he had taken from the prisoner.

"What's your name?" I asked.

"Fritz Freireich" he answered wearily.

The MP's took Freireich to the military prison; it was too late for me to interrogate him that evening. Joachim wanted me also to also arrest his sister, because she had tried to help her brother's escape. I was tempted, but decided against it. She would have had to be tried in a German court; no local jury would have convicted her.

That night I had my recurring nightmare: Nazis coming to take several children and me to a concentration camp. When I woke up, my bed in its usual disarray, I thought with pleasure of Freireich's arrest and looked forward to his interrogation.

My office, where the interrogation took place, was simply furnished: A desk, several chairs, two file cabinets and an old couch. I did have several pictures on the walls, all reproductions, except for a Käthe Kollwitz lithograph that I had bought in Berlin. Theatrics were now officially frowned upon. Furthermore they would no longer have worked. Individuals brought in for questioning knew very well that they would not be physically mistreated.

I asked the policemen who brought Freireich to my office to wait while I interrogated him. He sat in front of me with an air of self-assuredness that I found hard to accept. Most of the questioning was uneventful. He readily admitted that he had been a Gestapo official, that he had interrogated French resistance members, though he denied torturing any. I did not press the point; I knew the French would try him on that charge and assumed that they could produce witnesses. The man had answered all my questioned with a nonchalance that bordered on the arrogant. My level of acute vexation rose continually.

"Did you ever arrest any Russian agents?" We were now instructed to ask that question because CIC headquarters, then located in Frankfurt, wanted to get a feeling for the degree of Soviet penetration of German intelligence operations.

"A few," he almost had a smirk on his face. "And now I suppose you will ask our help to catch the ones who are spying on you." The answer, perhaps because I realized that it contained more than just a kernel of truth, infuriated me.

Then I started asking him about the report that he had sent to their death many Jewish children. He made no bones about the deal he had made with the mayor of the town.

"The arrest of all Jews was ordered by Berlin. You follow orders too don't you?"

The bastard really knew how to get to me.

"Anyway, the mayor reneged on his side of the bargain. He hid two Jews, adults, on his farm. When I found out about that I was really mad and arrested the children".

So a moment of pique had caused he death of fifty children.

"Fifty? Oh no. We could only find twenty eight of the little darlings."

Something snapped in me. I went over to his chair and slapped Freireich's face as hard as I could. He looked at me insolently but did not say anything. One of the MP's told me to take it easy. I walked back to my side of the desk and forced myself to sit down.

After I calmed down somewhat I said to the Gestapo agent: "I have already notified the French war crimes officer that we have arrested you. You will be taken to Frankfurt in a few days and there turned over to the French. What they do with you from the on is their business. Personally, I hope that they hang you."

"I suppose they will. The winners hang the losers. I have one request, as one soldier to another. My wife and children live in Hanover, only a few kilometers from here. I haven't seen them in over two years. I hope that I will at least be permitted to have them come here, before you turn me over to the French."

"And how many of the Jewish children saw their parents before you had them murdered?"

I gave strict orders that the man was to be kept in isolation until transport to Frankfurt was arranged. As I turned him over to the MP's I said to one of them: "You know I have interrogated many of these swine but this is the first one I ever touched."

The soldier gave me an odd look. "I have a girlfriend here; that's why I reenlisted. So I speak pretty good German, enough to understand what this guy said. I didn't see you hit nobody."

Freireich didn't complain about my slap, surely not worth mentioning in his lexicon, and was turned over to the French. I heard that he was tried, convicted of having tortured prisoners to death and ordered to be hanged.

Did he get to see his family before his execution? I have no idea. In the following years, after I returned to the US, I often thought about the incident. Should I have permitted a visit by his wife and especially his children? After I became a father I thought that no matter what the man had done, keeping him from seeing his children was too cruel. Did I descend to his level?

In 1964 I was invited to spend a summer working in a Dutch health laboratory outside The Hague. By then I had become a biophysicist, appointed to the faculty of Stanford University, working on Cancer problems. I had come with my wife and three children. We had bought a car, a brown Landrover, and spent considerable time driving around the outskirts of the city attempting to find the park and camp where I had stayed in 1939. I could not remember its location. We almost gave up looking, when one Sunday quite by accident we came to the entrance of the park. I recognized it instantly. We drove to the building, now gleaming in its recently painted whiteness. No nuns appeared this time. Instead, a young man with long curly blond hair came out the side door. We got out of the car to talk to him.

My Dutch had deteriorated to the point where I much preferred English.

"What is this building?"

"It's a youth hostel" his English was quite good.

"Do you have any idea of its previous history?" I asked.

"It burnt down during the war." For Europeans in the sixties World War II was still The War. "Only recently has the government found the money to rebuild it."

"And before the war?"

"I was told that some German Jewish refugee children lived here. They were trying to escape the Nazis. I understand they were all killed during the German occupation. But this was before my time."

I told him that there was at least one survivor. He was quiet for a second, obviously not knowing what to say, then he invited me in to see the building, "as it is today," but I declined. I was already being flooded with too many memories. My family watched me in silence as I paced up and down in front of the building. Pictures of children floated in front of my eyes, and I could hear their voices:

little Erna, confident Hertha, Heinz and Eva and other faces and tones that no longer had names.

After a while it was too much. I could not stand it any more. I went into the car and started the motor. As my wife and children climbed into the vehicle, another face appeared before me: that of Fritz Freireich. At that moment I was quiet sure that I had done the right thing in not letting that monster see his family. No punishment was severe enough for the killers of the children.

2003: Epilogue.

I was only on the periphery of the Holocaust. I did not experience the gruesome trip in the cattle cars that carried my aunts to the gas chambers nor the was I forced to endure the horrors of the camps. Slow starvation killed my grandmother, but in Holland I encountered hunger only because I was so spoiled that I did not want to eat the unappetizing Dutch food. I cannot even call myself a survivor, that would be an insult to the real survivors. I was a refugee, an uprooted person. The ship that took me to America and the one that returned me to Europe in wartime crossed the oceans without mishap so that I did not suffer the watery death that killed my two Romanian cousins. Except for a few black eyes, a slap in the face, neither my sister nor I were physically harmed. My mother suffered extreme mental anguish worrying about her husband and her children, and I came perilously close to losing my emotional balance; but of my immediate family only my father came face to face with the naked expression of Nazi pathopsychology.

Nevertheless the black scourge that had its origin in the hearts of millions of Germans and Austrians profoundly changed my life. Their hatred of Jews robbed me of much of my childhood and the events resulting from that hatred introduced a seemingly insurmountable barrier between my father and me. For years I felt that I, as a black haired, black-eyed Jew, must be inferior to all blond, blue eyed Aryans who seemed destined to conquer the world. Never mind that my eyes were and are just as blue as theirs and that my hair was brown, like that of many Germans. I felt like a Jew, like the kind of Jew caricatured in the vicious Nazi literature. For a long time I thought that the only way I could circumvent my heritage was to deny it. Rational thought was eliminated from both sides of the imaginary racial equation; from them, the self proclaimed supermen, and from us, their eternally damned sub-humans. It was only after I had interrogated many sniveling, frightened, lying, obsequious ex-supermen that my psyche came to terms with the vicious absurdity of racial ideology.

After the war, when the full extent of German atrocities and mass murder became known, I, like so many others who managed escape, was subject to an acute and long lasting attack of guilt. But in my case, not only did I carry the burden of the living, but I had also a nagging feeling that while in the army I should have done more to fight the Nazi enemy. Why did I not become a commando, killed SS-men, slit the throats of Gestapo interrogators, and if needed, get killed trying? Did I let others fight for me?

Some years after the war, I met another Jewish escapee, also an ex-Viennese, who then lived in Honduras. Our conversation quickly turned to a favorite topic among Jewish émigrés: What was special about us? What was it in our background that enabled us to escape against all odds? Why were we allowed to live when so many perished? To play the devil's advocate, I pointed to my father's will to live, to my mother's strength and determination to leave Europe, to the help we had from relatives that lived outside Germany.

My new acquaintance, who was a few years older than I was, shrugged. "Yes, the things you mentioned were of considerable importance in many cases." He obviously was not impressed by my suggestions.

"What was it then?" I asked? "Do you think that God picked you and me?"

"Look, I'll tell you how I got out. I had a school acquaintance, I wouldn't even call him a friend, who studied mining engineering. I knew him primarily as a bridge partner. He, incidentally, was not a Jew. To my parents' disgust we spent quite a bit of time at the game. They kept telling me that I was wasting my time and should study more, like my three brothers. He, the fellow card player, went to work for a British company that operated mines all over the world and was sent to a silver mine in an isolated area of northern Honduras. There the entire technical staff consisted of himself and two other European engineers. Life in the lonely mountains was very boring and they desperately needed a fourth for bridge. So they convinced the company's management that the mine needed an administrator and that I was the man. I knew nothing about mining, spoke no Spanish, but on their recommendation the company hired me sight unseen and sent me money for my fare. The Honduran government issued me a visa and I spent the war years playing cards in the rugged mountains of Central America. My three brothers, two were older and the other, my twin brother, my beloved Kurt, did not get out. They, and my parents, all died. To this day I don't even know where. My brothers and I were all rather similar; none of us was either a fool nor a genius. The only characteristic that set me apart from them was my ability to play Bridge. And that's what saved my life. The idea that some superior being chose me over my brothers

I find both repugnant and arrogant. Repugnant, because I can't believe that any deity could be so ruthless and capricious as to make such choices and arrogant because it would suggest that in some way I was better in the eyes of God than the other members of my family. I can only conclude that it was luck and luck alone that saved my life."

In spite of my earlier comments, I had long ago come to the same conclusion. In 1938, a close friend of mine was on his way to England. He was flying to London, and for reasons that I can't remember, he had to fly via Berlin. While sitting in that citiy's airport, waiting for his connection, an official of the German airline announced that effective immediately Jews would be required to have special, written permission from the Gestapo to go on a plane with a foreign destination. Of course my friend did not have such a document. He was faced with the prospect of having to return to Vienna and perhaps never again getting the chance to leave. A German Army officer, who happened to be sitting next to him in the waiting room, could not help but to notice his consternation. A remarkable, and totally unexpected thing happened.

"We look quite a bit alike;" the officer said to my friend. "You take my passport and get out of this country. Tomorrow I'll say that I lost it. Nobody is going to harm me." A rare and brave act by the officer who did not even know my friend.

So my friend reached England. Planning? Personal perseverance? Help from foreign relatives? No, just plain luck. When faced with a cataclysm of incredible magnitude such as the holocaust or the unthinkable bloodletting of war, man's individual actions amount to very little. My escape from the canisters of Zyklon B was the direct result of events totally out of my control or that of my family. My mission to parachute into Germany and very likely die in the attempt to establish contact with the anti-Hitler forces evaporated not because of anything I did but because of historical events that I did not even know about. Those of us who eluded the fate the Nazis had in store for us, or survived the killing fields of the battlefronts, did so because we held the right lottery ticket. Those who didn't perished.

About the Author

George Hahn was born in Vienna in 1926. After Austria was annexed by the Germans in 1938, he fled, first alone to the Netherlands, where he spent a year in a children's camp, and finally, after the outbreak of WWII, with his family to the United States. Towards the end of WWII and for some time afterwards he was an American Counter Intelligence agent. Later he attended the University of California in Berkeley and Stanford University, where he studied Biophysics. Hahn was appointed to the faculty of the Stanford School of Medicine 1966. He has written or co-authored four books and over 200 articles. Currently he lives with his wife in Carmel Highlands, California.

Printed in the United States
130355LV00002B/161/A